THE GREAT SEAL OF THE STATE OF CALIFORNIA

EUREKA

FAMILY AND FRIENDS

James A. Banks, Ph.D.

Kevin P. Colleary, Ed.D.

Stephen F. Cunha, Ph.D.

Jana Echevarria, Ph.D.

Walter C. Parker, Ph.D.

James J. Rawls, Ph.D.

Rosalía Salinas

Emily M. Schell, Ed.D.

 Macmillan McGraw-Hill

PROGRAM AUTHORS

James A. Banks, Ph.D.
Russell F. Stark University
Professor and Director, Center
  for Multicultural Education
University of Washington
Seattle, Washington

Kevin P. Colleary, Ed.D.
Curriculum and Teaching
  Department
Graduate School of Education
Fordham University
New York, New York

Stephen F. Cunha, Ph.D.
Professor of Geography
Humboldt State University
Arcata, California

Jana Echevarria, Ph.D.
Professor, College of Education
California State University
Long Beach, California

Walter C. Parker, Ph.D.
Professor of Education and
  Chair of Social Studies Education
University of Washington
Seattle, Washington

James J. Rawls, Ph.D.
Department of History
Diablo Valley College
Pleasant Hill, California

Rosalía Salinas
Senior Director
Learning Resources and Educational
  Technology Division (retired)
San Diego County Office
  of Education
San Diego, California

Emily M. Schell, Ed.D.
Social Studies Education Director,
City Heights Educational
  Collaborative
Visiting Professor, Teacher Education
San Diego State University
San Diego, California

California Geographic Alliance
Humboldt State University
Arcata, California

HISTORIANS/SCHOLARS

Steven Aron, Ph.D.
Professor of History
University of California,
Los Angeles and Executive
  Director, Autry National Center
Los Angeles, California

Amrik Singh Dua, Ph.D.
Professor and Department Chair
Department of Business
  Administration
Mount San Antonio College
Walnut, California

Paula S. Fass, Ph.D.
Margaret Byrne Professor
  of History
University of California
Berkeley, California

James M. McPherson, Ph.D.
George Henry Davis '86 Professor
  of American History, Emeritus
Princeton University
Princeton, New Jersey

Karen Nakai, Ed.D.
Professor, College of Education
California State University
Long Beach, California

Curtis C. Roseman, Ph.D.
Professor Emeritus of Geography
University of Southern California
Los Angeles, California

David Yoo, Ph.D.
Associate Professor of History
Claremont McKenna College
Claremont, California

CONSULTANTS
Primary Sources Research
Library of Congress
Publishing Office
Washington, D.C.

Reading and Writing
Adria F. Klein, Ph.D.
Professor Emeritus
California State University
San Bernardino, California

English Learners
Elizabeth Jimenez
Pomona, California

GRADE LEVEL CONSULTANTS AND REVIEWERS

Victoria Ford
Project Administrator
Monte Vista Elementary School
Montclair, California

Debra Gallagher
First Grade GATE
74th Street Elementary School
Los Angeles, California

Pamela McGregor
Project Coordinator, Teaching
  American History
San Diego County Office
  of Education
San Diego, California

Soma Varma
First Grade Teacher
Greenville Fundamental School
Santa Ana, California

Cynthia Vaughn
Elementary School Teacher
Rooftop Alternative School
San Francisco, California

CALIFORNIA EDITORIAL ADVISORY BOARD

Ginger Borror
Sixth Grade Teacher
Easterby Elementary School
Fresno, California

Tim Broader
Elementary Teacher, Grades 3-6
Susan B. Anthony
  Elementary School
Fresno, California

Kathleen Brown
Sixth Grade Teacher
Mitchell Community
  Elementary School
Santa Clarita, California

Stephanie Buttell-Maxin
Third Grade Teacher
Kimball Elementary School
National City, California

Dr. Tina Cantrell
Former Curriculum Director
Assistant/Associate Superintendent
Moorpark Unified School District
Moorpark, California

Marlene Dane
Third Grade Teacher
Bonita Canyon School
Irvine, California

Bev Farrell-Smith
Second Grade Teacher
Mitchell Community
  Elementary School
Santa Clarita, California

Victoria Ford
Project Administrator
Monte Vista Elementary School
Montclair, California

Debra Gallagher
First Grade GATE
74th Street Elementary School
Los Angeles, California

Michael Haggood
Principal
Los Angeles Unified School District
Los Angeles, California

Bill Laraway
Fifth Grade Teacher
Silver Oak Elementary School
San José, California

Sheri Nagel
Superintendent of Schools
Central School District
Rancho Cucamonga, California

Dr. Janet Scott
Principal
Peres Elementary
Richmond, California

Maria de los Angeles Villa
Second Grade Teacher
Roosevelt Elementary School
Pomona, California

Doua Vu
Resource Specialist
Office of State and Federal
  Programs/Title III
Fresno Unified School District
Fresno, California

Claudia West
Third Grade Teacher
Westlake Hills Elementary
Westlake Village, California

B

The McGraw·Hill Companies

Macmillan McGraw-Hill

Published by Macmillan/McGraw-Hill, of McGraw-Hill Education, a division of The McGraw-Hill Companies, Inc., Two Penn Plaza, New York, New York 10121.

Printed in the United States of America

ISBN 0-02-150508-X

3 4 5 6 7 8 071 10 09 08 07

★ CONTENTS ★

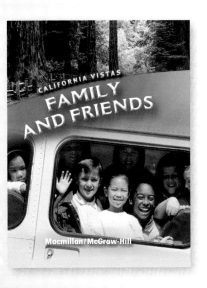

UNIT 1

Our World 1

Charts, Graphs, and Diagrams

Maps

Maps

Primary Source Quotations

CALIFORNIA STANDARDS

★ ☆ ★

You will see California standards on most pages of this book. California standards tell about important things to learn in social studies.

Look at the page below. It is the first page of a unit. Every unit helps you to meet a California standard.

This is where the California standard is.

UNIT

5

1.6 Students understand basic economic concepts and the role of individual choice in a free-market economy.

We Work

The Big Idea

Why do people work?

Painter on the Golden Gate Bridge in San Francisco

201

Explore The Big Idea

Every unit in your book has a Big Idea question. The Big Idea question helps you to learn about the topic of the unit.

You can find the Big Idea question on the first page of every unit.

This is the Big Idea question.

On the last page of every unit, there is a Big Idea Activity. It is a fun way to show all that you have learned about the Big Idea.

This is the Big Idea Activity.

Reading
Your Textbook

You can learn more about the Big Idea question on the Big Idea pages. These pages will help you get ready to read the unit.

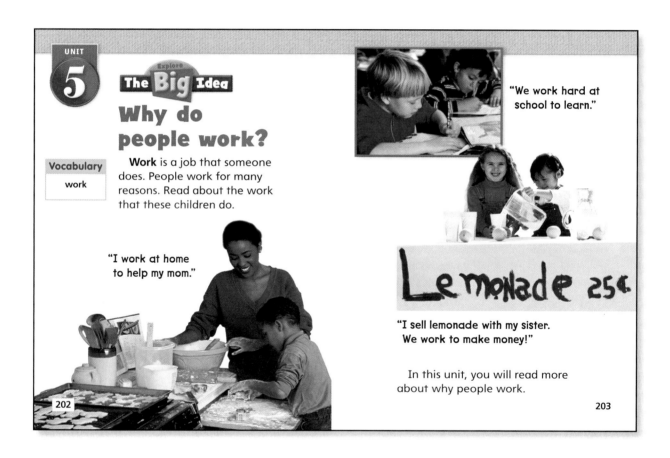

UNIT 5

The Big Idea
Explore

Why do people work?

Vocabulary
work

Work is a job that someone does. People work for many reasons. Read about the work that these children do.

"I work at home to help my mom."

"We work hard at school to learn."

Lemonade 25¢

"I sell lemonade with my sister. We work to make money!"

In this unit, you will read more about why people work.

202

203

UNIT 5 Literature

An Aesop's Fable

The Ant and the Grasshopper

retold by Noah Michaels
illustrated by Laura Huliska-Beith

Grasshopper loved to have fun. He liked to hop and sing. One day, he saw Ant.

204

UNIT 5 Vocabulary
About Economics

Read the words in the boxes. Look at the pictures. Learn what the words mean.

Goods are things that are made or grown for people to buy. (page 234)

Services are jobs that people do for others. (page 235)

208

▲ Each unit has a song, story, or poem.

▲ You will learn new vocabulary in each unit.

▼ Each unit has many lessons. You will learn new things in each lesson.

LESSON 1

1.6 Students understand basic economic concepts and the role of individual choice in a free-market economy.

Needs and Wants

Vocabulary

needs
shelter
wants

Things we must have to live are called **needs**. People need food to eat, water to drink, and clothes to wear.

People also need **shelter**. Shelter is a place where someone lives.

People need love and care, too. Families and friends can help meet these needs.

★ Why do people need food and water?

212

213

Each unit will help you to learn new skills. Skills lessons help you learn about maps, charts, graphs, and reading social studies.

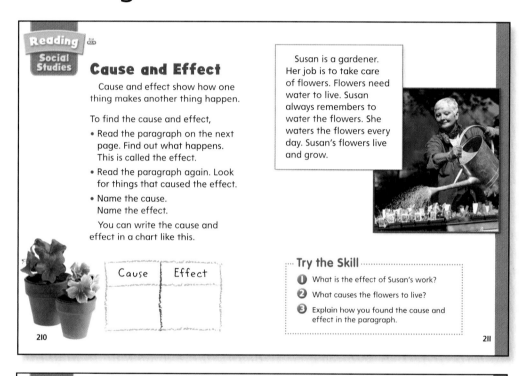

Reading Social Studies

Cause and Effect

Cause and effect show how one thing makes another thing happen.

To find the cause and effect,

- Read the paragraph on the next page. Find out what happens. This is called the effect.
- Read the paragraph again. Look for things that caused the effect.
- Name the cause. Name the effect.

You can write the cause and effect in a chart like this.

Cause	Effect

Susan is a gardener. Her job is to take care of flowers. Flowers need water to live. Susan always remembers to water the flowers. She waters the flowers every day. Susan's flowers live and grow.

Try the Skill

1. What is the effect of Susan's work?
2. What causes the flowers to live?
3. Explain how you found the cause and effect in the paragraph.

210

211

Chart and Graph Skills

Use Picture Graphs

A **picture graph** uses pictures to show numbers of things. The title tells you what the picture graph shows.

Sally and Beth sold glasses of lemonade for one quarter each. On which day did they sell the most lemonade? Look at the picture graph on the next page to find out.

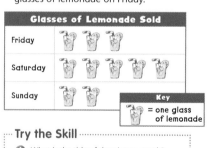

The key shows you that one glass stands for one glass of lemonade. Count the glasses next to the word *Friday*. There are three. Sally and Beth sold three glasses of lemonade on Friday.

Glasses of Lemonade Sold	
Friday	🥤 🥤 🥤
Saturday	🥤 🥤 🥤 🥤 🥤
Sunday	🥤 🥤

Key
🥤 = one glass of lemonade

Try the Skill

1. What is the title of the picture graph?
2. On which day did Sally and Beth sell the most lemonade?
3. **Activity** Make a picture graph to show that Sally and Beth sold six glasses of lemonade on Monday.

222

223

There are also lessons about being a good citizen. Some lessons tell about the lives of important people.

Cooperation and Compromise

Sometimes we do not agree. When this happens, we try to find ways to solve our problem. **Cooperation** is when people work together.

Here are two apples.

But there are four of us.

One way we can work together is to **compromise.** A compromise is a way we solve a problem. Each person gives something up. Each person also gets something.

I want my own apple.

We can cut them so we can all share.

Citizenship Activity

Tell a story about a time when you made a compromise with a friend.

238

239

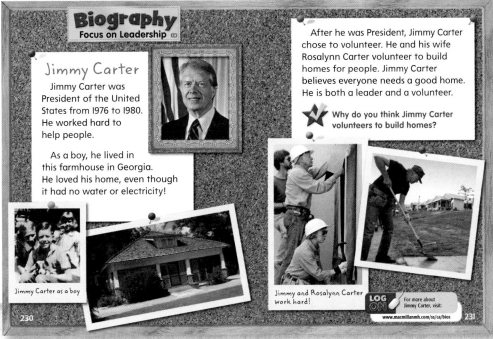

Jimmy Carter

Jimmy Carter was President of the United States from 1976 to 1980. He worked hard to help people.

As a boy, he lived in this farmhouse in Georgia. He loved his home, even though it had no water or electricity!

After he was President, Jimmy Carter chose to volunteer. He and his wife Rosalynn Carter volunteer to build homes for people. Jimmy Carter believes everyone needs a good home. He is both a leader and a volunteer.

Why do you think Jimmy Carter volunteers to build homes?

Jimmy Carter as a boy

Jimmy and Rosalynn Carter work hard!

LOG ON For more about Jimmy Carter, visit:
www.macmillanmh.com/ss/ca/bios

230

231

Geography Handbook

A Letter from Stephen Cunha

Dear Students:

Hi. I am Stephen Cunha. I am one of the authors of this book. I teach geography. **Geography** is the study of places and people.

You will read about geography in this handbook. You will also learn about maps. You will see how geography is a part of your life!

Stephen Cunha

Stephen Cunha
The California Geographic Alliance

The Five Themes of Geography

You can think of geography in five parts. Each part is a theme. These themes help us to learn about geography.

Location

A location tells where a place is on Earth. Your home address is a location.

Place

There are many kinds of places on Earth. Roads, cities, and mountains are all places.

Region

A region is a bigger area than a place. A region shares the same weather and landforms.

Movement

There is movement when people go from place to place. The ways that people move can change the land and air.

People Change the Land

People build roads, houses, and parks. The things people build change the land.

Dictionary of Geographic Words

Hill– land that is higher than the land around it, but lower than a mountain

Lake– body of water with land all around it

Mountain– a very high area of land

River– long body of water that flows across the land

Plain– flat land

Ocean– large body of water

Reviewing Geography Skills

Models and Maps

Look at the model of the playground. A model is a small copy of a place or object.

Look at the map of the playground. A map is a drawing of a place. A map shows how a place might look from above.

A Playground

How is the map like the model?
How is the map different from the model?

Photos and Maps

Look at the photo on this page. It is a picture from the air. It shows a neighborhood. You can see that the neighborhood has many houses on a street.

Now look at the map of the neighborhood on this page. Can you find the houses and the street?

A Neighborhood

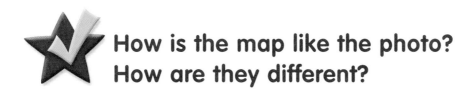

How is the map like the photo?
How are they different?

Picturing Earth

Earth is our home. It is round, like a ball. This is a picture of Earth. It is taken from outer space. The blue areas are oceans. The orange and green areas are land.

Earth

This is a model of Earth. It is called a globe. It shows what the land and water look like on Earth.

The equator is a line around the middle of the globe. It divides Earth into two equal parts: North and South.

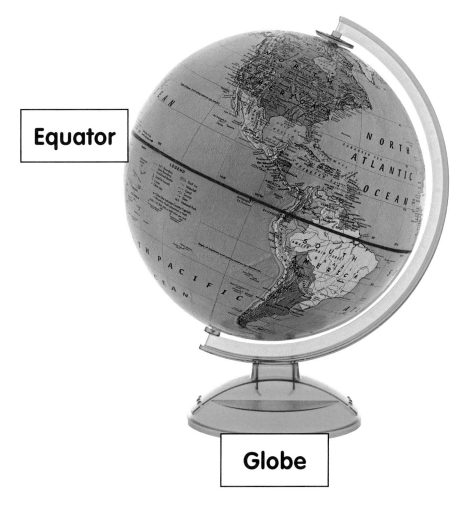

Equator

Globe

 What does the globe show?

Our World

The **Explore** Big Idea

How do we learn about geography?

View of Mount Shasta in California

Explore
The Big Idea

How do we learn about geography?

Vocabulary

geography

Geography is the study of places. There are many ways we can learn about geography.

"A globe can help me learn about geography."

"I can visit places to learn about them."

In this unit, you will learn more about geography.

"I can look at pictures of faraway places."

Country Cousin, City Cousin

retold by Matilda Ruiz
illustrated by
Gideon Kendall

Meet City Cousin. He lives in the big city. He likes the *honk, honk, honk* of the cabs. He likes the *tap, tap, tap* of little feet as city mice hurry down the street.

But City Cousin is tired. He needs a rest. He knows where he will go. "I will visit my cousin in the country. I can rest there because it is quiet," he says.

Country Cousin is happy that City Cousin has come to visit. The cousins swim in the pond. They eat their favorite cheese.

Soon it is time for bed. They can hear the *hoot, hoot, hoot* of the owl. They can hear the *croak, croak, croak* of the frog.

Country Cousin falls asleep. City Cousin is wide awake.

"It sure is noisy in the country," thinks City Cousin. "I need to go back to the city. Now city sounds do not seem noisy at all!"

Talk About It! What do you think might happen if Country Cousin went to the city to visit City Cousin?

Vocabulary

About Geography

Read the words in the boxes.
Then look at the pictures.

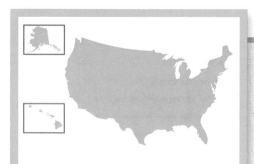

A **country** is a land and the people who live there. (page 28)

ARCTIC OCEAN

GREENLAND

ALASKA (U.S.)

CANADA

UNITED STATES

ATLANTIC OCEAN

MEXICO

N
W E
S

A **globe** is a model of Earth. (page 26)

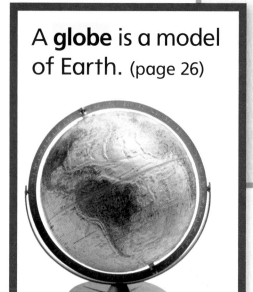

An **ocean** is a large body of water. (page 32)

A **city** is a big and busy place where people live. (page 18)

Write About It! What do you see in these pictures?

9

Find the Main Idea and Details

The **main idea** tells what a story is about. The details give more information.

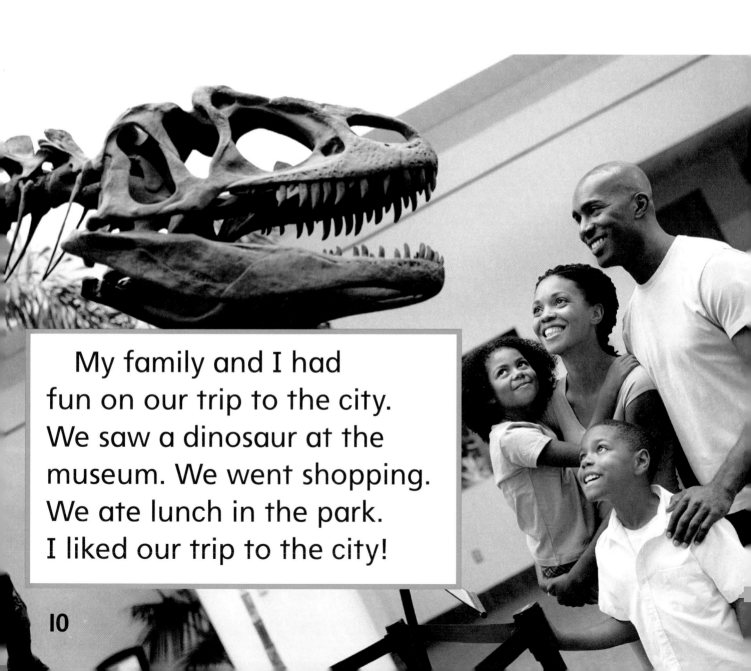

My family and I had fun on our trip to the city. We saw a dinosaur at the museum. We went shopping. We ate lunch in the park. I liked our trip to the city!

To find the main idea,

1. Read the story.

2. Decide what the story is about. This is the main idea.

3. Read the story again. Details tell you more about the main idea. Find the details of the story.

You can write the main idea and details in a chart like this one.

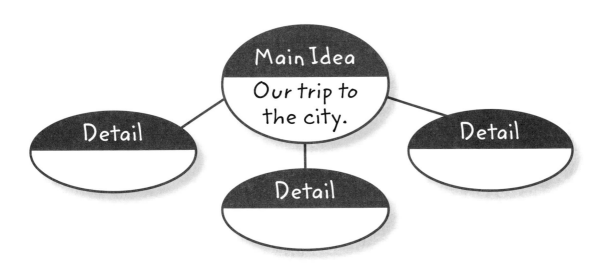

Try the Skill

1. What is the main idea of this story?

2. What are the details of this story?

3. What does the main idea tell?

I.2 Students compare and contrast the absolute and relative locations of places and people and describe the physical and/or human characteristics of places.

Around the Neighborhood

Vocabulary

neighborhood

address

absolute location

Welcome to the **neighborhood**! A neighborhood is a place where people live. Neighborhoods can be big or small.

Neighborhoods have many buildings. A neighborhood can have a playground and a school. It can have a store and a post office.

 What is a neighborhood?

Find an Address

People need to find places in the neighborhood. Each building has an **address**. An address tells the number and street name of a place. An address is an **absolute location**. It tells the exact spot where a place is.

Look at the house in the picture below. Its address is 2 Elm Street. Find this house on the map on the next page.

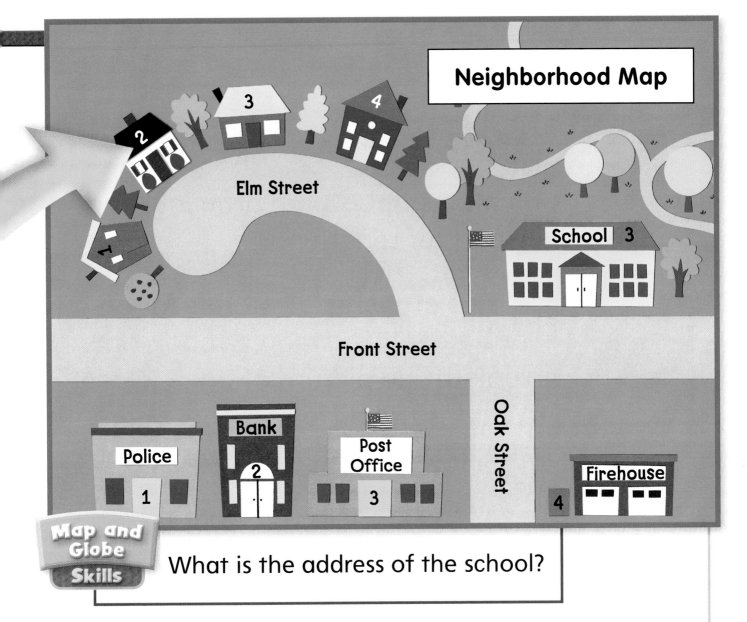

Neighborhood Map

Elm Street

3

4

2

1

School 3

Front Street

Oak Street

Police 1

Bank 2

Post Office 3

Firehouse 4

Map and Globe Skills

What is the address of the school?

How does an address help us?

Lesson Review

1. What is an absolute location?

Big Idea 2. What does the map tell you about this neighborhood?

3. **Find the Main Idea and Details** What places can you find in most neighborhoods?

Use a Map Key

Map **symbols** are drawings that stand for real things.

This drawing 🌳 stands for an oak tree. It is a map symbol. Now look at the picture of an oak tree. What is the difference between the picture and the map symbol?

A **map key** tells you what the symbols on a map mean. Find the bench symbol on the map on the next page. Now point to a bench on the map.

···Try the Skill···

1. What is next to the 🛝 in the map?

2. What does the map symbol 🛝 stand for?

3. **Activity** Draw a map of a place you know. Include map symbols and a map key.

Park Map

Map Key

Oak Tree

Slide

Bench

Swings

1.2 Students compare and contrast the absolute and relative locations of places and people and describe the physical and/or human characteristics of places.

City, Suburb, and Town

Vocabulary

city

suburb

town

relative location

There are many kinds of neighborhoods. A neighborhood can be in a **city**. A city is a big and busy place where people live. A city may have tall buildings.

City

A neighborhood can be in a **suburb.** A suburb is near a city. A suburb may have rows of houses. A suburb can be a quiet place to live.

Suburb

A neighborhood can be in a small **town.** A small town is far from the city. A small town may be near farms.

How is a small town different from a city?

Small town

Relative Location

One way to find a place is to tell its **relative location**. Relative location tells what is near a place.

Look at the picture below. The suburb is near the city. Can you find the suburb?

A farm is far from the city.
Can you find a farm?

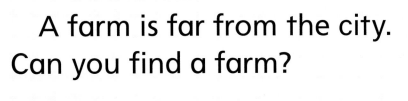

What is near the city?

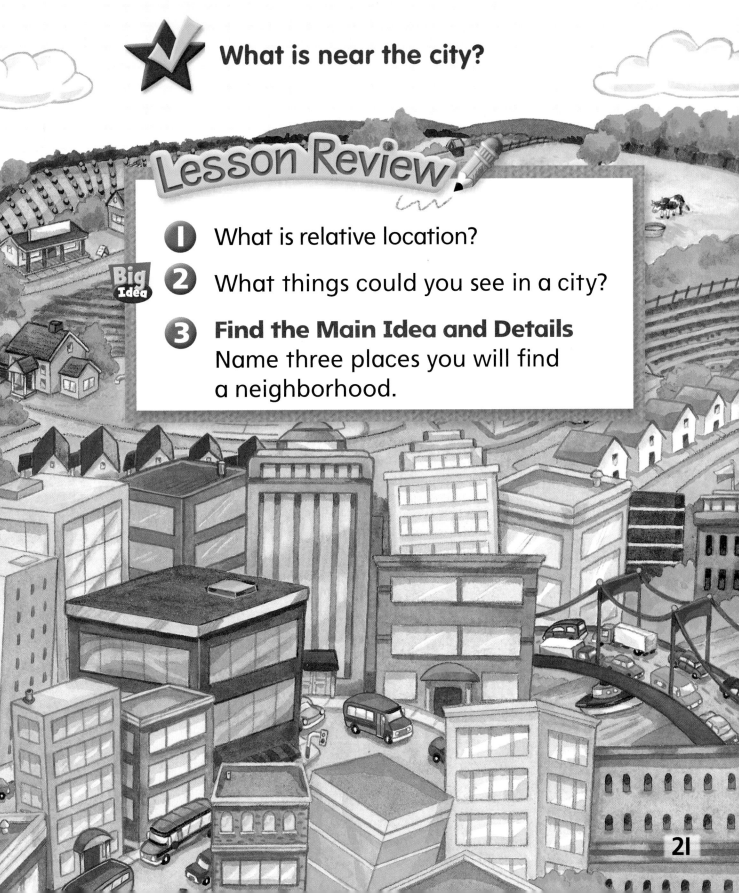

Lesson Review

1. What is relative location?

Big Idea 2. What things could you see in a city?

3. **Find the Main Idea and Details**
Name three places you will find
a neighborhood.

SEQUOIA NATIONAL PARK

GENERAL SHERMAN

Come along on a trip to the Sequoia National Park in California. This park has the biggest trees in the world. We call these trees Giant Sequoia.

Look at this huge tree. It is named General Sherman. This is the tallest tree in the park!

Sequoia
National Park

This is the trunk of a Giant Sequoia. Twenty people can hold hands around it!

Here is a log tunnel. A tree fell down. A tunnel was made through it!

What is the tallest tree in the park?

LOG ON

For more about Sequoia National Park, visit:

www.macmillanmh.com/ss/ca/fieldtrips

1.2.4 Describe how location, weather, and physical environment affect the way people live, including the effects on their food, clothing, shelter, transportation, and recreation.

Places Change

Places change with time. These two pictures show the same place.

The picture below shows how the place looked long ago. Long ago, the place had few houses. There was a lot of open space.

San Jose long ago

This picture shows how the place has changed. Many people have moved here. Now there are many buildings. There is little open space.

San José today

Lesson Review

1. How has the place changed with time?

Big Idea

2. What can you learn about the place from the picture taken long ago?

3. **Compare and Contrast** Find one way that the place has stayed the same. Find one way the place has changed.

Use Maps and Globes

Maps and globes help us to learn about our world.

Look at the **globe** on this page. A globe is a model of **Earth**. Earth is the planet we live on.

Earth is nearly round. The globe shows us the shape of Earth. You can spin a globe and see every part of Earth.

Look at the map on this page. All maps are flat. A world map shows you all of Earth at one time. A map makes it easy to find places all over the world.

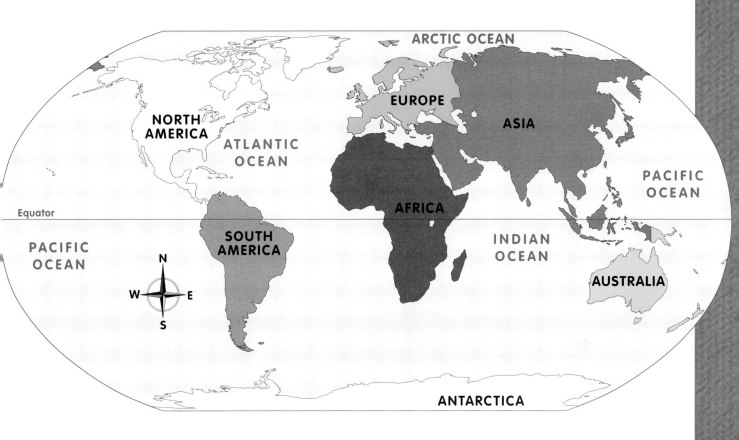

Try the Skill

1. What does a globe show us about Earth?

2. What does a map make it easy to do?

3. **Activity** Find North America on a world map. Then find North America on a globe.

I.2.I Locate on maps and globes their local community, California, the United States, the seven continents, and the four oceans.

Our Country, Our Earth

Your neighborhood is in a **state**. A state is part of a country. We live in the state of California.

This map shows our **country**. A country is a land and the people who live there.

The name of our country is the United States of America. Our country has 50 states.

How many states are in our country?

Map and Globe Skills

Can you find the state of California on the map?

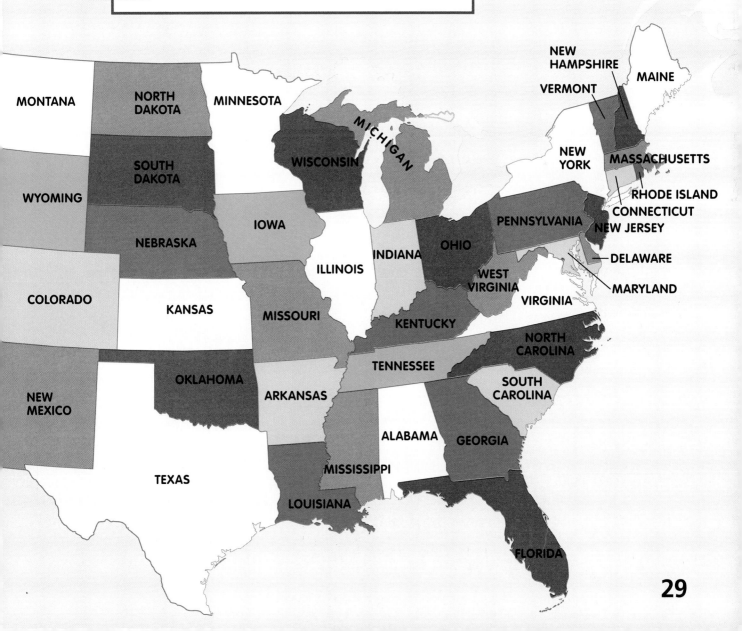

Our Country's Neighbors

Our country is part of a **continent.**
A continent is a large body of land.
Our continent is called North America.

Our country has two neighbors.
They are Mexico and Canada.

Canada

Mexico

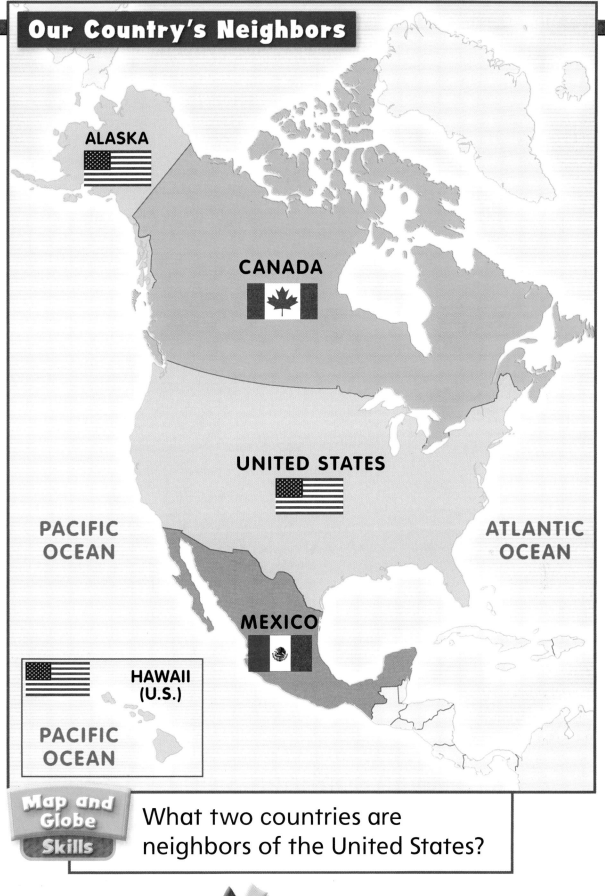

ALASKA

CANADA

UNITED STATES

PACIFIC OCEAN

ATLANTIC OCEAN

MEXICO

HAWAII (U.S.)

PACIFIC OCEAN

Map and Globe Skills

What two countries are neighbors of the United States?

What is a continent?

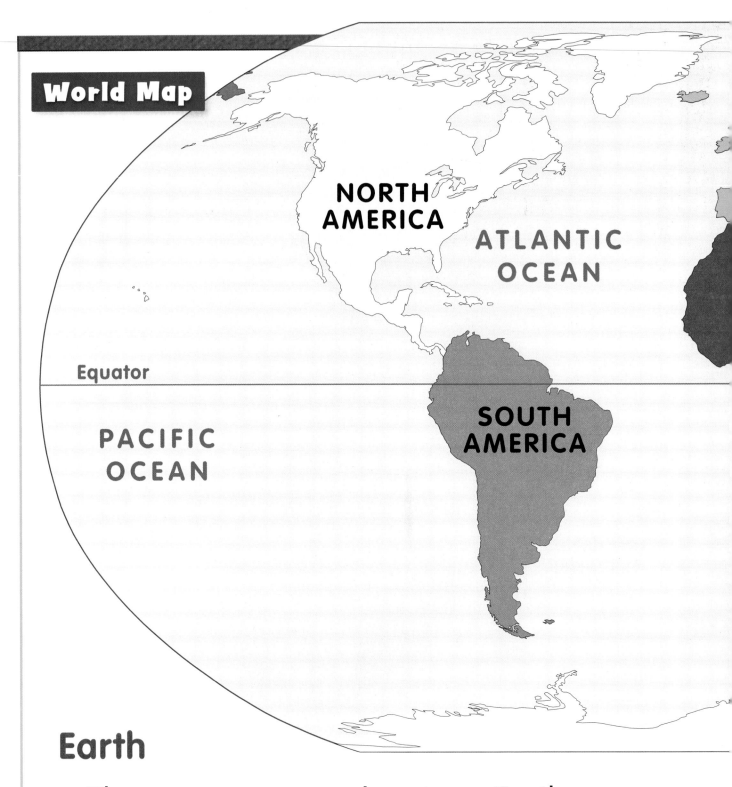

NORTH
AMERICA

ATLANTIC
OCEAN

Equator

PACIFIC
OCEAN

SOUTH
AMERICA

Earth

There are seven continents on Earth. The continents are North America, South America, Europe, Asia, Africa, Australia, and Antarctica. Earth has four **oceans**. An ocean is a large body of water.

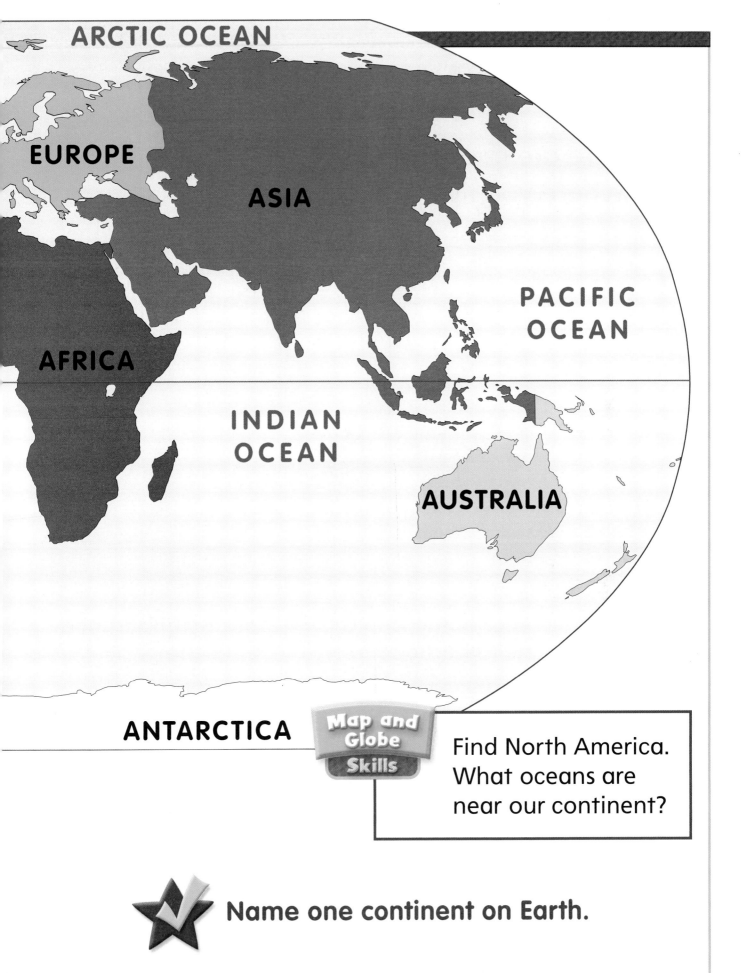

ARCTIC OCEAN

EUROPE

ASIA

AFRICA

PACIFIC OCEAN

INDIAN OCEAN

AUSTRALIA

ANTARCTICA

Map and Globe Skills

Find North America. What oceans are near our continent?

Name one continent on Earth.

Where You Live

There are many names for where you live.

You live in a home.

Your home is in a neighborhood.

Your neighborhood is in a state.

 Where is your state?

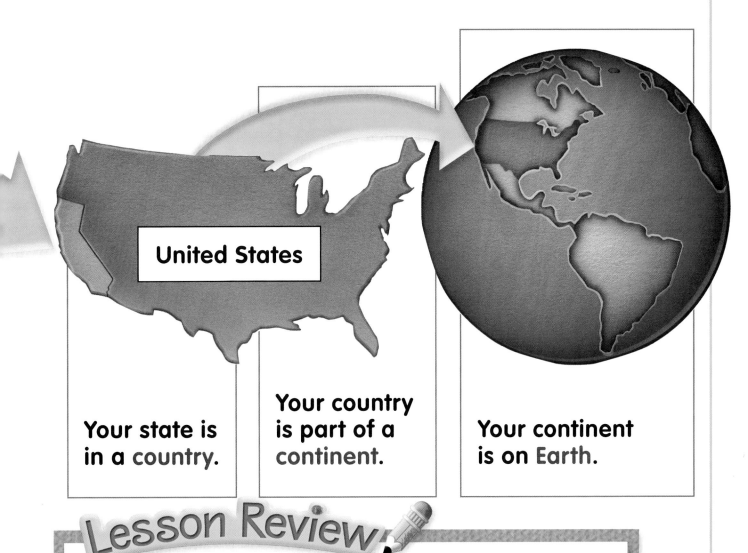

United States

Your state is in a country.

Your country is part of a continent.

Your continent is on Earth.

Lesson Review

Big Idea

1. How many continents are on Earth?

2. Name your state, country, and continent.

3. **Find the Main Idea and Details** Reread pages 34 to 35. What is the main idea? What are the details?

Celebrate Our World with a Song

Big Beautiful Planet

Words and Music by Raffi

There's a   big beauti-ful plan-et in the sky, _____

And it's my home, _____ It's where I   live.

36

Write a song about where you live.

F   Gm   F

You and man - y oth - ers live here too. _____

Gm   F

The earth is our home, ___ it's where we live. _____

Good Citizens Care for the World

We care about how we treat others. We care about our world, too. Look at these pictures. What would you do?

Joe

I don't need this!

Emily

Please stop! Don't make someone else pick up your trash!

38

How is Emily being a good citizen? How is she helping to take care of our world?

Being a Good Citizen

Tell how you care about the world.

Activity

A classmate trips over some toys on the floor. Draw a picture to show how you could help.

1.2.4 Describe how location, weather, and physical environment affect the way people live, including the effects on their food, clothing, shelter, transportation, and recreation.

Weather and Seasons

Weather is what the air is like outside. The weather is not the same everywhere. One place might be sunny. Another place might have rain.

Our country is big. The weather is different in different places. People have fun in every kind of weather.

California

Bob lives in California. It is sunny there. Bob can play outside all year.

California

Vermont

Vermont

Jasper lives in Vermont. It is cold there in winter. He likes to play in the snow.

What is weather?

Four Seasons

In some places, the weather stays the same all year long. In other places, the weather changes with the **seasons**. The seasons are the four parts of the year. They are spring, summer, fall, and winter.

Spring

Summer

People can do different things each season.

 What things do you do each season?

Winter

Fall

 Lesson Review

1 Name the four seasons.

Big Idea **2** What are the seasons like where you live?

3 **Compare and Contrast** How is summer different from winter?

Rachel Carson

Rachel Carson grew up on a farm near a river. Her mother taught her to love the land, air, and sea.

Rachel became a scientist. She studied birds, fish, and other living things.

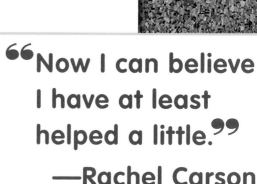

Using Primary Sources

"Now I can believe I have at least helped a little."

—Rachel Carson

Rachel Carson looked at soil from different places. When the soil was clean, the plants grew better.

Rachel wrote a book about what she learned. She showed that we need to take care of Earth.

 How did Rachel Carson show she cared about Earth?

Soil A

Soil B

Rachel Carson taking soil samples for testing.

For more about Rachel Carson, visit:

www.macmillanmh.com/ss/ca/bios

1.2.4 Describe how location, weather, and physical environment affect the way people live, including the effects on their food, clothing, shelter, transportation, and recreation.

Living in Alaska

Meet Sarah! Sarah lives in Alaska. It is very cold there. Sarah wears thick clothes to keep warm.

In winter, the sun shines very little. It is dark even when Sarah wakes up! The sky is filled with stars.

Barrow, Alaska

Sarah likes to go to school. After school, she plays with her dogs. Their names are Star, Dash, Snowball, Max, Rocket, and Lightning.

 Where does Sarah live?

Sarah loves the weekend. She has fun with her family. They like to go dogsledding. The dogs pull the sled. They go fast across the ice.

Sarah is glad her family lives in Alaska. She loves her home!

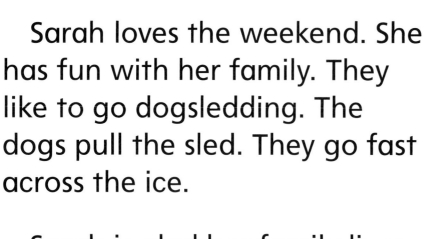

 What does Sarah do on the weekend?

Lesson Review

1 What does Sarah see in the winter when she wakes up?

Big Idea **2** How is Sarah's life different from yours?

3 **Summarize** What does Sarah love about life in Alaska?

Geography in Spain

Andorra Mountains

Spain is a country on the continent of Europe. Spain has sandy beaches, mountains, and even a desert. A desert is a dry place where few plants grow.

Moor

The weather in Spain is like the weather in California. It is warm and mild most of the time.

Majorca Beach

Spanish House

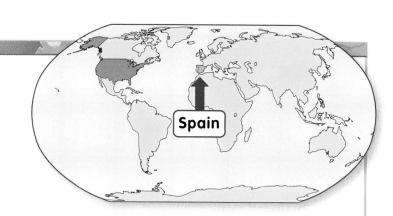

Spain

Many homes in California look like houses in Spain. There is a good reason for this. Long, long ago, people from Spain moved to California. They built homes like the ones they had in Spain.

Barcelona

Write About It! How are California and Spain alike?

Review

Find the Main Idea and Details

Read the paragraph about how to find a place. Then answer the questions.

Jane lives in a city. A city is a busy place with many people. Jane loves living in a city. Her home is on a high floor of a tall building. She likes to play with her neighbors. She loves riding the bus to school. She enjoys all the sights and sounds of a city.

1 What is the main idea of this paragraph?

2 Find two details that tell what Jane loves about her life in a city.

3 What is weather?

4 What is the word for a land and the people who live there?

5 What is a continent?

Critical Thinking

6 Why is it good to know your address?

7 What might you wear in the winter?

8 Write about the neighborhood that you live in.

I.2

Look at the map and map key below. Then use the map and map key to answer the following questions.

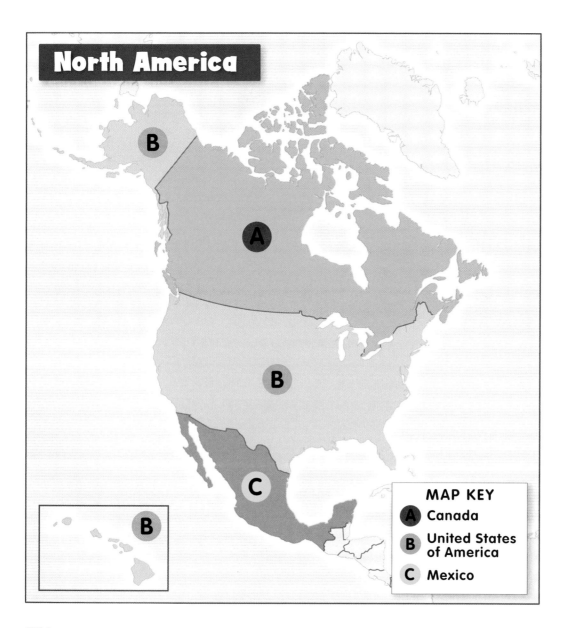

North America

MAP KEY
A Canada
B United States of America
C Mexico

1 Which letter on the map stands for the United States of America?

A A

B B

C C

D D

2 What country does "C" stand for?

A North America

B Mexico

C Canada

D United States of America

3 What continent does the map show?

A North America

B Africa

C Australia

D Europe

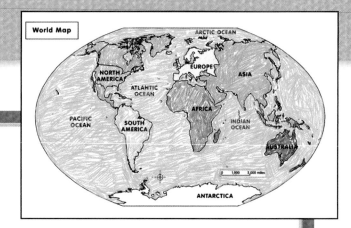

World Map

Color a World Map

1. Your teacher will give you a copy of a world map. Color the oceans blue.

2. Trace each of the seven continents in its own color. Do not use blue.

3. Find California on the world map. Draw a house in the part of California where you live.

4. Show your world map to a friend!

Read More About the Big Idea

To learn more about geography, you can read one of these books.

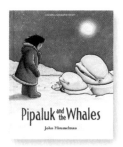

Pipaluk and the Whales
John Himmelman

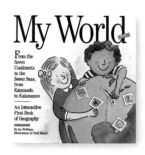

For help with the Big Idea activity, visit:
www.macmillanmh.com/ss/ca/launchpad

UNIT

2

I.I Students describe the rights and individual responsibilities of citizenship.

Good Citizens

The Explore Big Idea

What makes a good citizen?

Good citizens help.

The Explore Big Idea

What makes a good citizen?

A **citizen** is a person who belongs to a country. These children show how they are good citizens.

"I clean up after myself."

"I help other people."

"I raise my hand before talking."

In this unit, you will learn how you can be a good citizen.

UNIT 2 Literature

We Are Good Helpers

by Sonia Munoz

illustrated by Keiko Motoyama

We are good helpers every day.
We put our books and toys away.
We feed our class pet, Goldie, too.
We help a lot. That is what we do.

We help to keep our classroom clean.
We are polite and never mean.
We help our classmates every day—
With reading, math, and when we play!

Talk About It! How can you help out?

Vocabulary
About Citizenship

Read the words in the boxes. Then look at the pictures. Learn what the words mean.

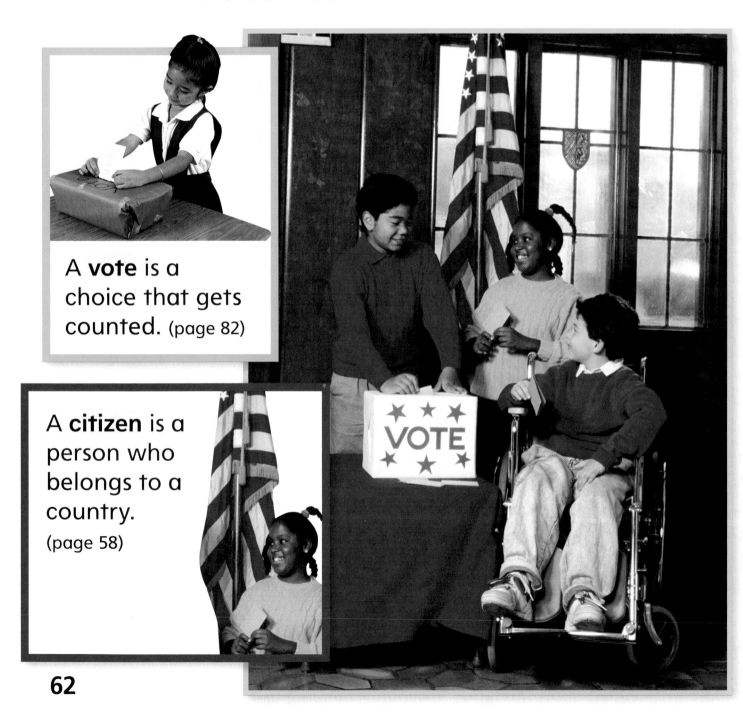

A **vote** is a choice that gets counted. (page 82)

A **citizen** is a person who belongs to a country.

(page 58)

A **community** is a group of people who live in the same neighborhood.
(page 76)

A **mayor** is the leader of a community.
(page 90)

Write About It! What do you see in these pictures?

Make Predictions

A **prediction** is a guess about what will happen next.

To make a prediction,

- Read the paragraph on the next page.
- Think about what you read and what you know.
- Use the information to guess what will happen next.

You can put your information in a chart like this.

What I Know	What I Predict

Read the paragraph below about the class. Then try the skill.

Our art teacher makes rules. One of the rules is to wash our paintbrushes when we are finished with them. In the morning some children forgot to wash their paintbrushes. The paintbrushes will not be used again until the afternoon.

Try the Skill

1. Why is it important for the class to wash their paintbrushes?

2. What do you predict will happen when the children try to paint in the afternoon?

3. What information did you use to make your prediction?

1.1.2 Understand the elements of fair play and good sportsmanship, respect for the rights and opinions of others, and respect for rules by which we live, including the meaning of the "Golden Rule."

We Belong

Did you know that you are part of a **group**? A group is made up of many people.

Your class is a group. A sports team is also a group.

Your family is a group, too. People in a group need to get along. That way, they can all have fun!

What are two groups that you belong to?

We Get Along

There are many ways that we can get along. We can listen to one another. We can help one another. We can share with one another. These are ways of showing **respect**. Respect is concern for others.

I feel left out.

My classmates are nice!

We show respect to everyone.
When we play games, we play fair.
We are kind when we win.
We are kind when we lose.

 What is respect?

1 How do we show respect when we play games?

Big Idea **2** How can we get along?

3 **Make Predictions** What might happen when people do not show respect to each other?

Ask a Friend

Mrs. Ramsey's class is in Morrisville, North Carolina. There are many helpers in Mrs. Ramsey's class. Mrs. Ramsey always says, "Before you come to me, ask a friend for help."

Vuong Le

Chamara Fernando

70

Jill Goodtree likes to help with reading. She says, "I help people to learn new words and how to say them."

Morrisville, North Carolina

Jill Goodtree

Being a Good Citizen ★

What are some other ways to help in the classroom?

Draw a picture of how you help people in your class. Write a sentence below your picture.

Use Charts

Charts use words and pictures to show things. The title tells you what the chart is about. This chart shows the jobs Katie does at home.

Read the top row of the chart on the next page. It names the kinds of jobs Katie does at home.

Put your finger on the word *Sunday*. Now move your finger across the chart. The **X** on the chart means that Katie feeds her cat on Sunday.

Katie's Jobs at Home

Day of Week	Set the Table	Put Away Toys	Feed the Cat
Sunday			X
Monday	X		X
Tuesday		X	X
Wednesday	X		X
Thursday		X	X
Friday			X
Saturday			X

Try the Skill

1. What days does Katie set the table?

2. What job does Katie do every day?

3. **Activity** Make a chart of the jobs you do at home.

LESSON

2

I.I.2 Understand the elements of fair play and good sportsmanship, respect for the rights and opinions of others, and respect for rules by which we live, including the meaning of the "Golden Rule."

All About Rules and Laws

Vocabulary

rule

community

law

Rules tell us what to do.
They help us to stay safe.
They help us to be fair.

Mr. Bing's
Classroom Rules
1. Raise our hands to talk.
2. Wash our hands before eating.
3. Throw our trash in the trash can.
4. Listen to our friends.

One rule is to raise your hand in class. This shows respect to your teacher. Another rule is to wash your hands. This helps keep you healthy.

 What are some rules in your class?

All About Laws

We follow rules in our **community**, too. A community is a group of people who live in the same neighborhood. A rule in a community is called a **law**. Laws tell us what we can and can not do. Everyone must follow them.

Laws help us to stay safe. It is a law to wear a helmet when you skate. It is a law to take care of our pets. It is a law to follow street signs. These laws help people in a community get along.

 Name a law that keeps you safe.

Lesson Review

1 What is a rule?

Big Idea 2 Why is it a rule to raise your hand in class?

3 **Summarize** How do rules and laws help us?

Use Directions

Directions tell us which way to go. North, south, east, and west are directions. These directions help us to find places.

Point to the arrow on the map that says south. Move your finger toward the arrow that says north. What direction are you traveling? If you said north, you are right!

Point to the arrow on the map that says west. Move your finger toward the arrow that says east. What direction are you traveling? If you said east, you are right!

Neighborhood Map

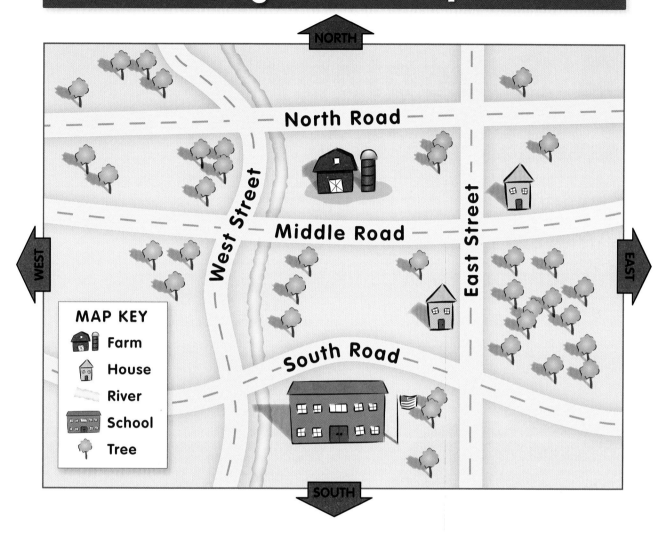

Try the Skill

1. Point to the farm. What direction do you travel to get to the school?

2. Point to East Street. What direction do you travel to get to West Street?

3. **Activity** Draw a map of your classroom. Include arrows to show the four main directions. Add a map key.

A Schoolboy Long Ago

Meet Charles! He lived in America long ago. Find out what his school day was like.

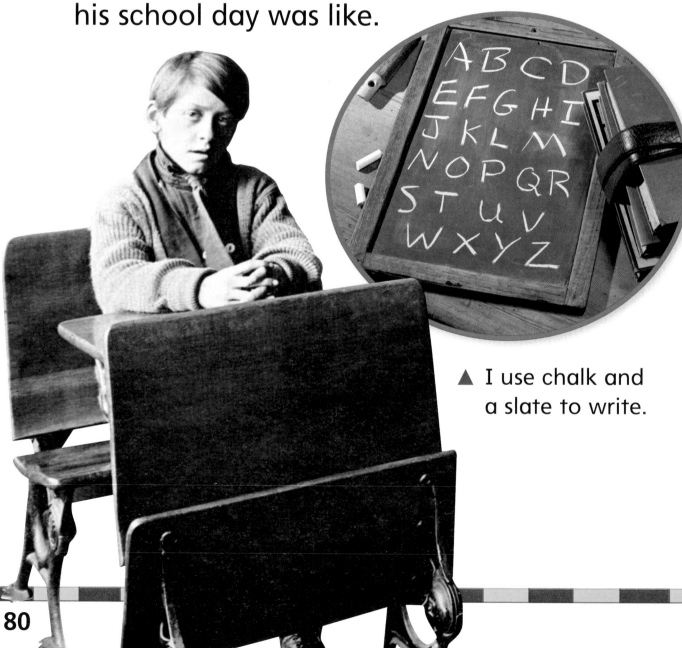

▲ I use chalk and a slate to write.

▲ My school has only one room.
We sit at wooden desks.

▲

My teacher rings a
bell when recess ends.

▼ I carry my lunch
in a pail.

Write About It! How was school different long ago?

LOG ON For more about life
in the 1800s, visit:

www.macmillanmh.com/ss/ca/dayinthelife

LESSON 3

I.I.I Understand the rule-making process in a direct democracy and in a representative democracy, giving examples of both systems in their classroom, school, and community.

Votes Count!

Sometimes we want to do different things. How do we decide what to do? We **vote**. A vote is a choice that can be counted. Everyone in the class gets one vote. A vote is a way of being fair.

82

Your class might vote to name the class pet. You might like the name Fluffy. Your friend might like the name Doodles. Your class can vote to choose the best name.

 What is a vote?

Leaders in Our School

A **leader** is a head of a group.
The teacher is the leader of a class.
The teacher makes the rules.

Children can be leaders, too. They
can lead a school project. They can
lead a sports team. Classmates can
vote for their leaders.

Children can become school leaders. They can work with teachers to make a better school. They can even run for school president!

 Who is the leader of your class?

Lesson Review

1. Name something you might vote on in your class.

Big Idea

2. How can children be leaders?

3. **Make Predictions** Predict what it would be like to be a leader. What kind of group would you like to lead?

Using Primary Sources

Using Photographs

A photograph is a primary source. A **primary source** is a thing from the past that helps us learn. It tells us about the past.

Look at this photograph. It is from the past. At the time this photograph was taken, women could not vote. The women in this photograph worked to change this law. You can see from the photograph that they marched.

Look Closely

Look at this photograph. Look at the women's clothes. How can you tell that the photograph is from long ago?

I WISH MA COULD VOTE

Primary Source Review

1 What is a primary source?

2 What does the above photograph show?

3 Look at the sign. What do you think it means?

LESSON

1.1.1 Understand the rule-making process in a direct democracy and in a representative democracy, giving examples of both systems in their classroom, school, and community.

Voting in a Community

Citizens can help their community. They can make their community a better place.

Some citizens on Oak Street want to make a nice garden for their community. So they ask their community for help.

Next the community meets. They take a vote. Some vote **Yes** for the garden. Some vote **No** for the garden. The votes are counted. If most of the community votes **Yes,** the community will have a garden.

 How can people make their community a better place?

People Vote for Leaders

Citizens in a community vote for a **mayor**. A mayor is the leader of a community. Citizens vote for other leaders, too. They vote for the leaders of their state and country.

Governor of California Arnold Schwarzenegger

Mayor of Los Angeles Antonio Villaraigosa

Our leaders work for us. They make decisions for us. They work to keep us safe, healthy, and free.

 What is a mayor?

Lesson Review

1. What do leaders do?

2. Why is voting fair?

3. **Summarize** How do we choose a mayor?

Martin Luther King, Jr.

Martin Luther King, Jr., had great courage. He worked to make things fair.

MARCH ON WASHINGTON FOR JOBS & FREEDOM AUGUST 28, 1963

Using Primary Sources

"We have not yet learned the simple art of living together as brothers."

—Martin Luther King, Jr.

Long ago, black and white children went to different schools. It was the law. Martin Luther King, Jr., knew this law was not fair. He led marches. He made speeches. He helped change the law. Now all children go to school together.

 How did Martin Luther King, Jr., make things fair?

LOG ON For more about Martin Luther King, Jr., visit:

www.macmillanmh.com/ss/ca/bios

1.1 Students describe the rights and individual responsibilities of citizenship.

Rights and Responsibilities

Vocabulary

right

responsibility

Citizens in our country have many **rights**. A right is a thing we are free to do. We have the right to vote. We have the right to belong to a group. We have the right to laugh, and talk, and play.

Citizens also have **responsibilities**. A responsibility is a thing we must do. We must follow laws. We must go to school. We must keep our community clean.

We wear seat belts.

Good citizens care about their community. They follow laws. They take care of their responsibilities.

We clean up.

Lesson Review

1. What are some of our rights?

Big Idea 2. What makes a good citizen?

3. **Compare and Contrast** What is the difference between a right and a responsibility?

Goldilocks Learns the Golden Rule

Characters

**Baby Bear • Goldilocks
Mama Bear • Papa Bear**

Narrator: The "Golden Rule" means treating others the way you want to be treated. Goldilocks is staying with the three bears. The bears love Goldilocks. But Goldilocks does not follow the rules.

Baby Bear: Goldilocks, it is time for a talk.

96

Goldilocks: What is wrong?

Mama Bear: We want to share our house rules with you.

Goldilocks: Okay.

Baby Bear: Please make your bed every day.

Goldilocks: Okay. Do you have more rules?

Papa Bear: We know you love porridge. You must wash your bowl when you are done.

Goldilocks: I can do that.

Baby Bear: Now you know all our rules.

Goldilocks: I will be sure to follow them.

Narrator: And Goldilocks did follow the rules. Goldilocks and the bears lived happily ever after.

Write About It! How do rules help Goldilocks and the bears get along?

First Graders in Japan

In Japan, children bow to their teacher at the start of class. One child says, "Good morning," in Japanese. Then all the children say, "Good morning."

Children in Japan
wear uniforms at school.
In the afternoon they play.
When school is over, the children
go home and study and play.

Japan

Write About It!

How are children in Japan
like children in America?
How are they different?

Review

Make Predictions

Read the paragraph about Mrs. Jones' great idea. Then answer the questions below.

Mrs. Jones has two ideas for a special treat for her class. One idea is to have a Hat Day. Another idea is to have a Pajama Day. How will she choose the best idea? She decides to have her class vote. Ten children vote for Hat Day. Five children vote for Pajama Day.

1. Do you predict that the class will choose Hat Day or Pajama Day?

2. How did you make your prediction?

3 What is a mayor?

4 What is the word for a group of people who live in the same area?

5 What is the word for the head of a group?

Critical Thinking

6 How is voting a fair way for a group to make a choice?

7 Why is it important that people follow rules?

Write About It! 8 Write about a leader in your class.

1.1.2

Use Charts

Look at the chart below. Then use the chart to answer the following questions.

Jobs in Mrs. Smith's Class			
	Erase the Board	Put Away Books	Put Chairs in a Circle
Michael		X	
Julia	X		
Fernando			X

1. What is the title of the chart?

A Games in Mrs. Smith's Class

B Snacks in Billy's House

C Ways to Get to School

D Jobs in Mrs. Smith's Class

2 Who puts away the books in Mrs. Smith's class?

    A   Mrs. Smith

    B   Fernando

    C   Michael

    D   Julia

3 Who erases the board?

    A   Michael

    B   Julia

    C   Fernando

    D   Mrs. Smith

I would like it if a friend gave me a hug when I am sad.

Book of Golden Rules

I would like it if someone shared their book with me.

Make a Book of Golden Rules

1. Draw a picture of someone treating you the way you would like to be treated.

2. Write one sentence about your picture.

3. Your teacher will put your pictures into a *Book of Golden Rules*.

Read More About the Big Idea

To learn more about citizenship, you can read one of these books.

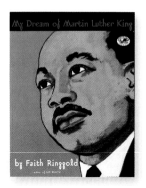

For help with the Big Idea activity, visit:

www.macmillanmh.com/ss/ca/launchpad

UNIT

3

1.3 Students know and understand the symbols, icons, and traditions of the United States that provide continuity and a sense of community across time.

America the Beautiful

The Explore Big Idea

How do we celebrate our country?

Statue of Liberty on July 4

How do we celebrate our country?

Vocabulary

celebrate

There are many ways to **celebrate** our country. To celebrate is to do something special.

"We celebrate our country by having parties on national holidays."

"We wave the flag to celebrate our country."

"We have parades to celebrate our country."

In this unit, you will learn more about how we celebrate our country.

America

This is a special song about our country. It is sometimes called "My Country 'Tis of Thee."

America

Music by Henry Carey
Words by Samuel F. Smith

My coun-try 'tis of thee, Sweet land of lib-er-ty, Of thee I sing. Land where my fa-thers died, Land of the Pil-grim's pride, From ev'-ry __ moun-tain-side Let __ free-dom ring.

Talk About It! What does the song tell us about our country?

Vocabulary

About Our Country

Read the words in the boxes. Look at the pictures. Learn what the words mean.

A **flag** is a symbol of a country. (page 114)

A **holiday** is a special day. (page 124)

To **celebrate** is to do something special.
(page 106)

A **monument** is a building or statue that helps us remember a person or an event. (page 136)

Write About It! What is happening in these pictures?

Summarize

When we **summarize**, we find a short way of saying something.

- To summarize, read the paragraph.
- Think about what the paragraph is about.
- Tell what the paragraph is about in one sentence only.

You can summarize in a chart like this.

Earth Day is...

Read the paragraph about Earth Day. Then try the skill.

Earth Day is a holiday. We celebrate Earth Day on April 22. Many people clean up their neighborhood on Earth Day. Earth Day is a time to think about the land, air, and water.

Try the Skill

1. Think about what you have learned about Earth Day.

2. Write down what you have learned about Earth Day.

3. Write one sentence to summarize the paragraph about Earth Day.

1.3.1 Recite the Pledge of Allegiance and sing songs that express American ideals.

1.3.3 Identify American symbols, landmarks, and essential documents, such as the flag, bald eagle, Statue of Liberty, U.S. Constitution, and Declaration of Independence, and know the people and events associated with them.

Vocabulary

symbol

flag

Symbols of Our Country

Our country has many **symbols**. A symbol is something that stands for something else. A **flag** is a symbol of a country.

The American flag has 50 stars. Each star stands for one of the 50 states.

We treat our flag with respect. We wave our flag. We pledge allegiance to it. To pledge allegiance means to promise to be loyal.

 What do the stars on our flag stand for?

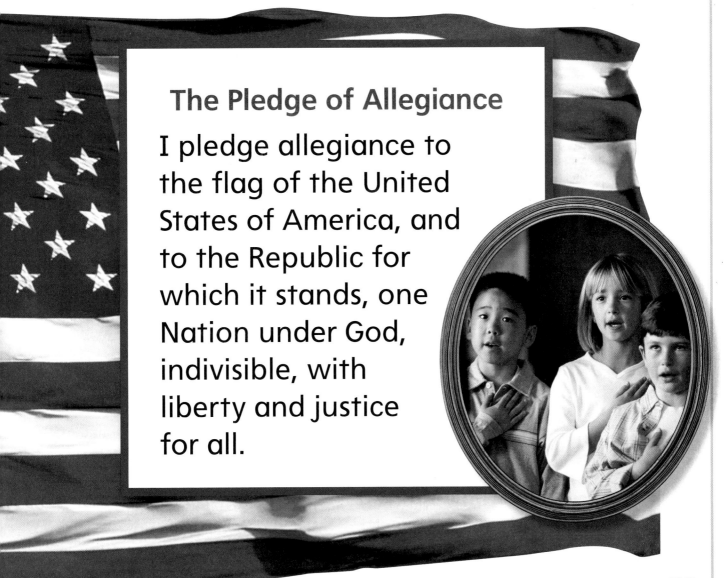

The Pledge of Allegiance

I pledge allegiance to the flag of the United States of America, and to the Republic for which it stands, one Nation under God, indivisible, with liberty and justice for all.

The Statue of Liberty

The Statue of Liberty is in New York City. It is a symbol of freedom. It is a symbol of hope, too. It welcomes people to our country.

There is a poem at the base of the statue. Emma Lazarus wrote it.

Emma Lazarus

Using **Primary Sources**

"Give me your tired, your poor, your huddled masses yearning to breathe free..."

—Emma Lazarus

The Statue of Liberty was a gift from France. It was built there long ago. It was sent to America on a ship.

The statue was too big to send in one piece. It was sent in more than 200 pieces!

The statue was put together in the United States. It took four months!

 What does the Statue of Liberty stand for?

The Bald Eagle

The bald eagle is a symbol. It stands for our country. It is big and strong. Our country is big and strong, too.

Presidential Seal

Bald eagle

It is easy to find pictures of the bald eagle. The bald eagle is on mailboxes. It is also on a quarter. You can even find the bald eagle on a space shuttle!

Mailbox

 What does the bald eagle stand for?

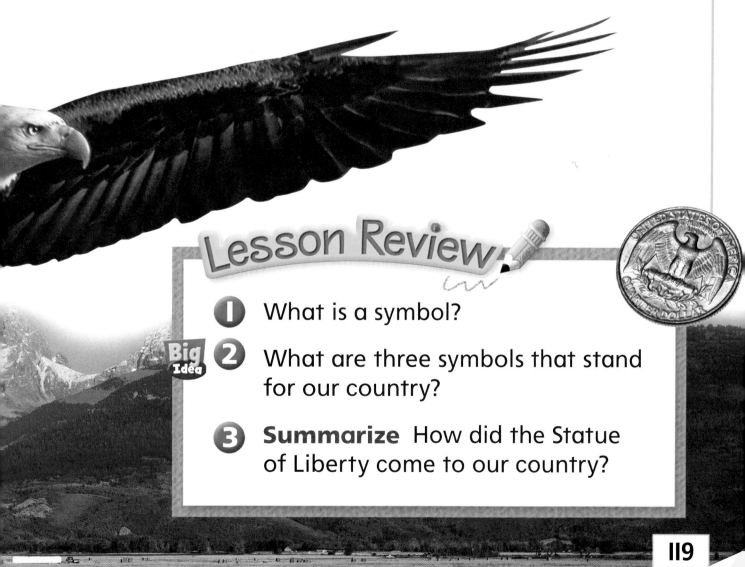

Lesson Review

1. What is a symbol?

Big Idea 2. What are three symbols that stand for our country?

3. **Summarize** How did the Statue of Liberty come to our country?

Locate Information

You can locate information about a book by looking at the book's cover. Look at the book cover on the next page.

The title is the name of the book. Find the title on the book cover.

The author is the person who wrote the book. Find the name of the author. The illustrator is the person who painted the pictures in the book. Find the name of the illustrator.

Title

Author

Illustrator

Try the Skill

1 Look at the book above. What is the title of the book?

2 Who is the author of the book?

3 **Activity** Look at another book in your classroom. Find the title, author, and illustrator.

1.3.2 Understand the significance of our national holidays and the heroism and achievements of the people associated with them.

Thanksgiving

Vocabulary

Native Americans

feast

holiday

Long ago, a small group of people left England. They were called Pilgrims. The Pilgrims wanted to be free. They came to North America on a ship.

The Pilgrims had a hard time at first. They did not have much food.

The Pilgrims arrive in North America.

122

Then **Native Americans** helped them. Native Americans were the first people to live in America. They showed the Pilgrims how to hunt and farm.

Soon the Pilgrims had a lot of food. They had a **feast** to give thanks to God. A feast is a large meal. The Pilgrims invited the Native Americans. This was the first Thanksgiving.

Why did the Pilgrims have a feast?

The first Thanksgiving

Thanksgiving Today

Today Thanksgiving is a **holiday.** A holiday is a special day. On Thanksgiving families and friends get together. People give thanks for what they have.

People celebrate this holiday in different ways. Many families have feasts. Some watch parades. Others watch football. What do you like to do on Thanksgiving?

 How do people celebrate Thanksgiving?

Lesson Review

1. Why did the Pilgrims come to America?

Big Idea 2. Why do we celebrate Thanksgiving?

3. **Summarize** Tell what happened when the Pilgrims came to America.

1.3

A Colonial Child

Meet Hope. She lived in America long ago. What was Hope's life like? Read more to find out!

I make candles. They give us light at night. ▶

◀ I stir the fresh milk.

I play games
with a hoop. ▶

◀ I love my doll.
I made it myself.

Write About It! How is Hope's life different from your life? How is it the same?

LOG ON For more about life
in the 1700s, visit:

www.macmillanmh.com/ss/ca/dayinthelife

1.3.3 Identify American symbols, landmarks, and essential documents, such as the flag, bald eagle, Statue of Liberty, U.S. Constitution, and Declaration of Independence, and know the people and events associated with them.

Independence Day

Vocabulary

independence

Long ago, America was not a free country. It was ruled by a country called England.

Many people in America wanted **independence**. Independence means freedom. So the leaders in America wrote the Declaration of Independence. It said that America wanted to be a free country.

American leaders sign the Declaration of Independence.

128

July 4, 1776 is the day the Declaration of Independence was signed. July 4 became known as Independence Day.

 What did the Declaration of Independence say?

The Declaration of Independence

A Free Country

England did not want America to be free. England and America went to war. The war was long and hard. At last, America won its independence.

George Washington led the American army.

Americans celebrate Independence Day on July 4. It is a holiday. We have picnics and parades. We show how happy we are to be free.

 Why do we celebrate Independence Day on July 4?

1. What country ruled America long ago?

Big Idea 2. Why do Americans celebrate Independence Day?

3. **Summarize** Tell how America won independence from England.

131

Use Historical Documents

The Declaration of Independence is a **document**. A document is a piece of paper with writing on it. This document is very old. It tells us about the past.

Look Closely

- Look at the document. This document tells why Americans wanted to be free.

- Find out when it was written. The date is at the beginning. It says *July 4, 1776.*

Date

Writing

Signatures

Primary Source Review

1 What is a document?

2 When was this document written?

3 Did one person or many people sign it? How can you tell?

Use a Diagram

A **diagram** shows the different parts of something. Look at the diagram on the next page. The diagram shows the parts of a printing press. The printing press was used to print papers.

Look at the part called the printing block. This is what presses ink on the paper. Look at the part called the wheel. This is what you turn to make the machine work.

The Declaration of Independence was printed on a printing press.

Printing block

Wheel

Paper

Try the Skill

1. Find where the paper goes in the printing press.

2. What does a diagram show?

3. **Activity** Make a diagram of your favorite toy.

1.3.3 Identify American symbols, landmarks, and essential documents, such as the flag, bald eagle, Statue of Liberty, U.S. Constitution, and Declaration of Independence, and know the people and events associated with them.

American Monuments

The United States has many **monuments**. A monument is a building or statue. A monument helps us to remember a person or event.

George Washington was the first President of the United States. People built the Washington Monument to remember him.

The Washington Monument

Vocabulary

monument

George Washington

Abraham Lincoln was the sixteenth President of the United States. He worked to make sure everyone in our country was free. The Lincoln Memorial helps us to remember him.

 How do we remember George Washington and Abraham Lincoln?

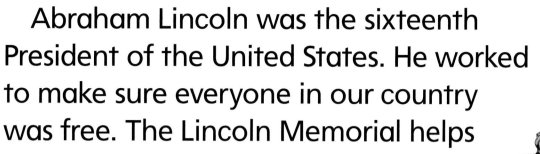

Abraham Lincoln

The Lincoln Memorial

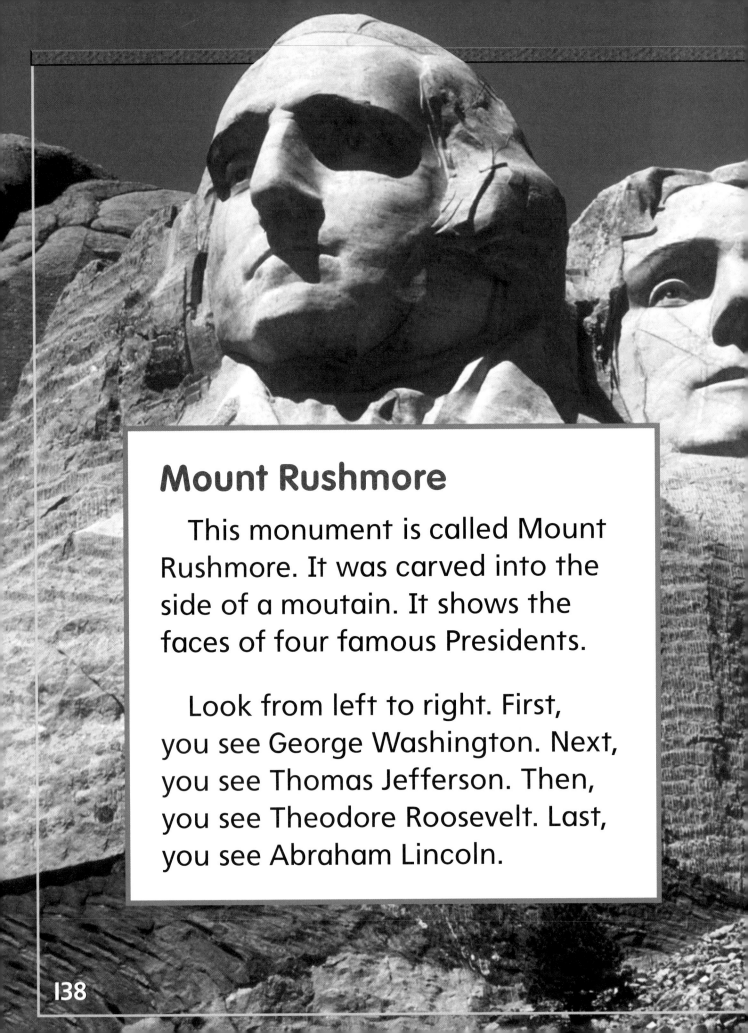

Mount Rushmore

This monument is called Mount Rushmore. It was carved into the side of a moutain. It shows the faces of four famous Presidents.

Look from left to right. First, you see George Washington. Next, you see Thomas Jefferson. Then, you see Theodore Roosevelt. Last, you see Abraham Lincoln.

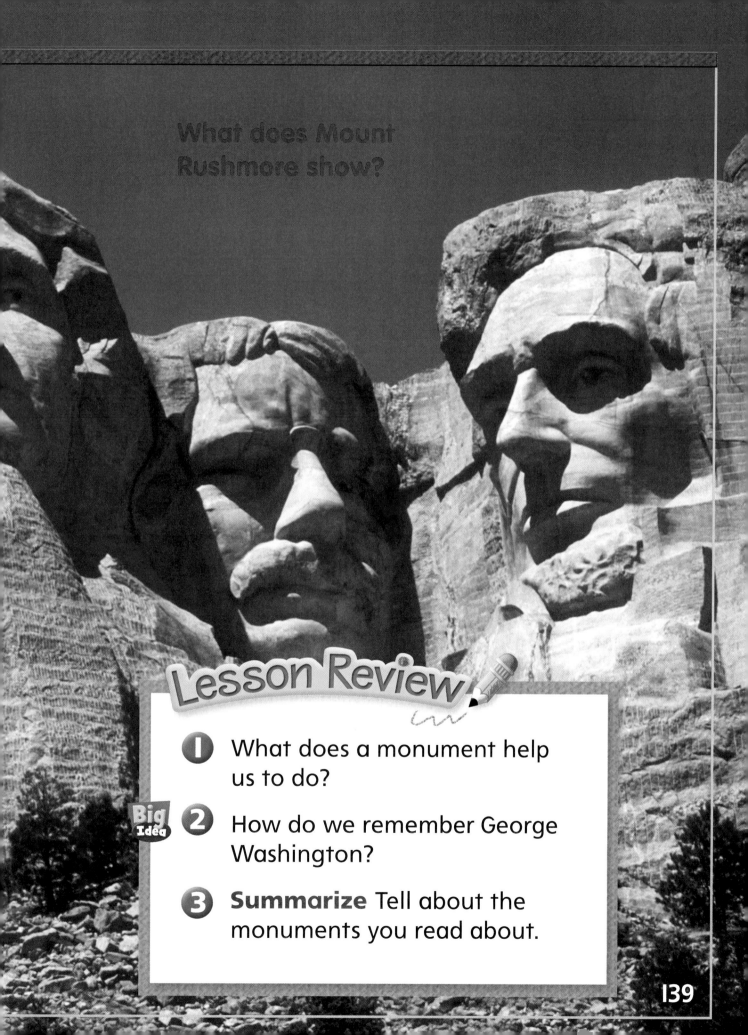

What does Mount
Rushmore show?

Lesson Review

1. What does a monument help us to do?

Big Idea 2. How do we remember George Washington?

3. **Summarize** Tell about the monuments you read about.

Abraham Lincoln

Abraham Lincoln was born in a one-room log cabin. His family was very poor. Abraham loved books. He once walked many miles in the rain to get one!

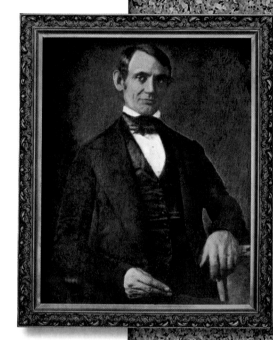

Using Primary Sources "The things I want to know are in books."
—Abraham Lincoln

Abraham Lincoln became the sixteenth President of the United States.

President Lincoln led our country during the Civil War. At that time, African Americans were not free. Abraham Lincoln helped African Americans become free.

Why was Abraham Lincoln a great leader?

Lincoln and his son

LOG ON For more about Abraham Lincoln, visit:

www.macmillanmh.com/ss/ca/bios

1.3.3 Identify American symbols, landmarks, and essential documents, such as the flag, bald eagle, Statue of Liberty, U.S. Constitution, and Declaration of Independence, and know the people and events associated with them.

A Plan for Our Country

Vocabulary

government

Long ago, the United States became a free country. It needed a plan for making laws.

The leaders of our country had a meeting. They made a plan. This plan is called the Constitution of the United States.

The U.S. Constitution

142

American leaders sign
the U.S. Constitution.

Our **government** follows the
Constitution today. The government
is a group of people who work for
all the citizens of a country.

Lesson Review

1. What is a government?

Big Idea 2. What is the Constitution?

3. **Summarize** Tell why the
Constitution was written.

Being Honest

Being honest means telling the truth. Sometimes it can be hard to be honest. Look at the story below. Find out what happened when Jane found a dollar.

I found a dollar today.

Sally lost a dollar today.

I will ask Sally if this is her dollar.

What is Jane going to do with the dollar? Is she honest? What would you do if you found a dollar?

Citizenship Activity

Draw a picture of a time when you were honest. What did you do?

Symbols in Kenya

Kenya is a country on the continent of Africa. Kenya has its own government, laws, and holidays. Each year Kenyans celebrate their freedom on June I.

Traditional dress

A monument to Kenya's first president

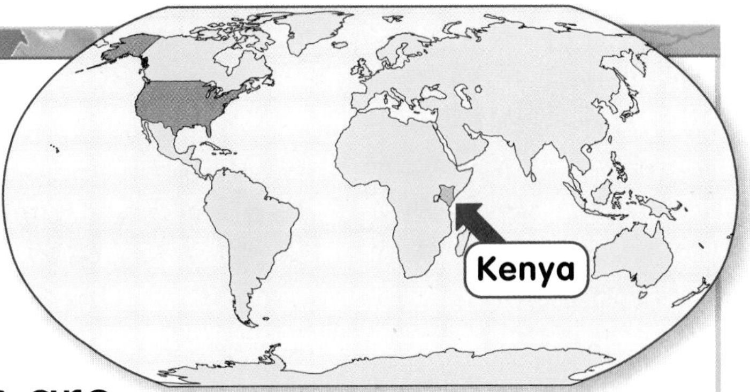

Kenya has a flag. The flag stands for independence. Its colors are black, red, green, and white. Kenya has monuments, too. The Independence Monument reminds Kenyans that they are free.

Kenya

Flag of Kenya

Independence Monument

Write About It! How are Kenya and the United States alike?

Summarize

Read the paragraph. Then answer the questions.

The United States flag shows many stars. Do you know how many stars are on the flag? There are 50 stars in all. Each star stands for one state. There are 50 states in our country. So there are 50 stars on our flag.

1 What does each star on the United States flag stand for?

2 Summarize the paragraph in one sentence.

Vocabulary

3 What is independence?

4 What is the word for a building or statue that helps us to remember history?

5 What is the word for a group of people who work for all the citizens of a country?

Critical Thinking

6 How does the Constitution help our country?

7 Why is independence important?

8 Write about why the Pilgrims needed help when they came to America.

1.3

Use a Diagram

Look at the diagram below. Then use the diagram to answer the questions.

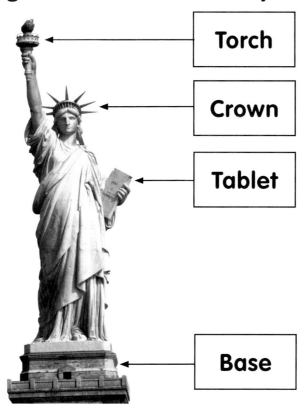

● What is on the head of the Statue of Liberty?

A a base

B a crown

C a tablet

D a baseball cap

2 What is the Statue of Liberty standing on?

    A   a crown

    B   a surfboard

    C   a base

    D   a tablet

3 What two things does the Statue of Liberty hold?

    A   a flag and an eagle

    B   a crown and a base

    C   a carrot and a rabbit

    D   a tablet and a torch

The Big Idea Activity

Make a Symbol Mobile

1. Think about symbols that are important to our country.

2. Draw pictures of three symbols.

3. Hang up your pictures.

Read More About the Big Idea

To learn more about our country's history, you can read one of these books.

For help with the Big Idea activity, visit:

www.macmillanmh.com/ss/ca/launchpad

1.4 Students compare and contrast everyday life in different times and places around the world and recognize that some aspects of people, places, and things change over time while others stay the same.

Now and Long Ago

Life was different long ago.

The Explore Big Idea

What was life like in the past?

Explore
The **Big** Idea

What was life like in the past?

Vocabulary

history

The past is a time long ago. **History** is what happened in the past.

Many things long ago were different. Some things are the same.

"Long ago, we went from place to place in different ways."

154

"Long ago, we lived in different houses."

"We played with toys long ago."

In this unit, you will read more
about what life was like in the past.

Literature

My Grandma and Me

by Nicole O'Neill
illustrated by Ed Martinez

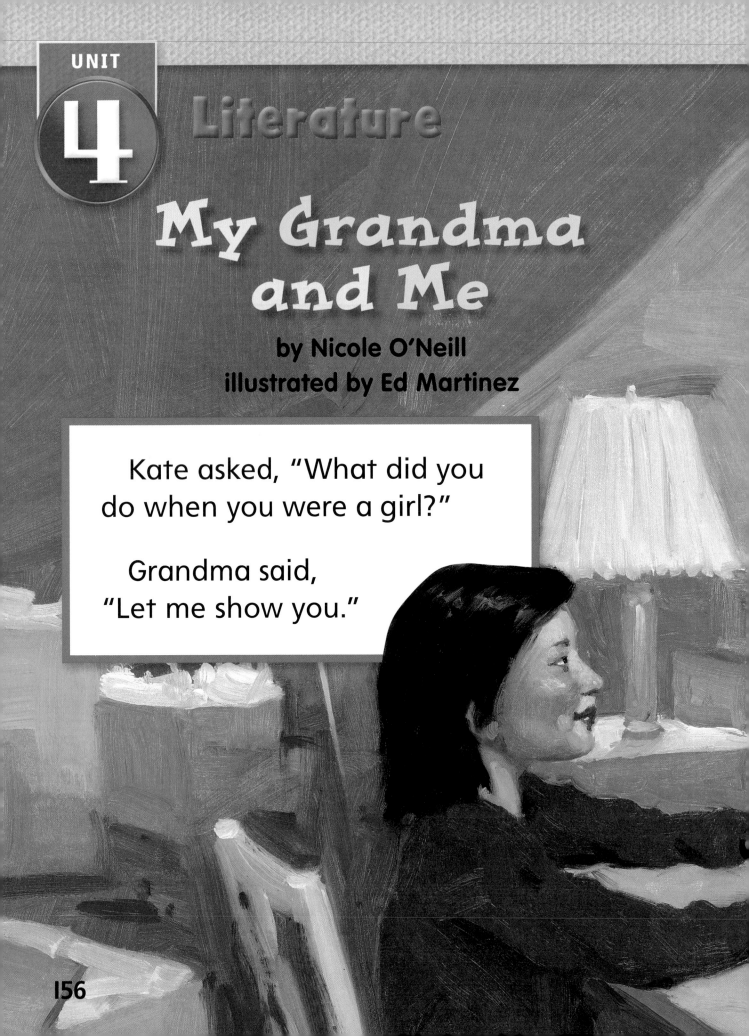

Kate asked, "What did you do when you were a girl?"

Grandma said, "Let me show you."

Grandma said, "I used this to write when I was your age."

Kate said, "It is different from our computer."

"I played records when I was your age," said Grandma.

"I like this music," said Kate.

Grandma said, "I liked to spend time with my grandma when I was your age. She told me about the past."

Kate said, "I like spending time with you, too."

Talk About It! Who tells you about the past?

Vocabulary

About History

Read the words in the boxes. Look at the pictures. Learn what the words mean.

A **library** is a place where you can read and borrow books.

(page 190)

A **museum** is a place that shows pictures and things from long ago.
(page 191)

Transportation is a way of moving people or things from place to place.
(page 182)

Write About It! What do you see in these pictures?

Put Things in Order

You put things in order when you tell what comes first, next, and last.

To put things in order,

- Read the story on the next page.
- Find out what happens in the beginning of the story.
- Find out what happens next in the story.
- Find out what happens last.

You can put things in order in a chart like this.

Put Things in Order	
First	
Next	
Last	

Read the story about taking a trip to the library. Then try the skill.

My class went to the library. First, we looked for books. Next, we took the books to a reading area. Last, we read the books!

First

Next

Last

Try the Skill

1 What does the class do first in the library?

2 What happens after the class looks for books?

3 Tell what happens first, next, and last.

I.4.3 Recognize similarities and differences of earlier generations in such areas as work (inside and outside the home), dress, manners, stories, games, and festivals, drawing from biographies, oral histories, and folklore.

All About the Past

Vocabulary

interview

There are many ways to learn about the past. One way is to look at family photographs. They can tell about your family's history.

My great grandma with my grandma and her baby sister

My mother as a child with her family

Look at the photographs. They show Ashley's family. The first photograph shows Ashley's grandmother when she was a little girl. The second photograph shows Ashley's mother when she was little. The third photograph shows Ashley and her mother today.

 Which family photograph is the oldest? How can you tell?

My mother and me

Interview Your Family

You can also learn about the past by talking to people. An **interview** is a conversation that you plan.

Keisha is interviewing her grandfather. She asks her grandfather questions about the past. Then Keisha writes the answers down.

Do you want to interview someone? Here is how.

My Grandpa

1. First, find a person you want to interview.

2. Next, make a list of questions.

3. Then, sit down with the person you want to interview. Ask your questions.

4. Last, write the answers down.

 Who is Keisha interviewing?

Lesson Review

1. What is an interview?

Big Idea 2. What are two ways that you can learn about the past?

3. **Put Things in Order** What are the steps you need to take for an interview?

Changing Every Day

by Rachel Geswaldo
illustrated by Martha Aviles

I'm getting bigger every day.

I'm growing up, you see!

I'm getting taller and
smarter, too!

My parents both agree.

I'll trade in my old tricycle
and get a brand new bike.

I'll make new friends
along the way,

And learn new things I like!

168

Crecer es un Placer

Cada día soy más grande.

Estoy creciendo,

me hago más alto, más listo.

Lo mismo piensan mis padres.

Ya ando en bici, adiós triciclo.

Tengo nuevos amigos.

Me gusta mucho aprender.

¡Crecer es un placer!

Activity

Write a poem about how you are changing. Tell how you stay the same, too.

Use Calendars

Calendars are charts. They show the months, weeks and days of a year. Calendars show holidays, too. Calendars help us keep track of time.

Look at the calendar on the next page. It shows the month of July.

Point to the square with the number four. It stands for one day, Tuesday, July 4.

Sunday	Monday	Tuesday	Wednesday	Thursday	Friday	Saturday
						1
2	3	4 Independence Day	5	6	7	8
9	10	11	12	13	14	15
16	17	18	19	20	21	22 Clean the Park Day
23	24	25	26	27	28	29
30 Dad's Birthday	31					

Try the Skill

1. How many days are in July?

2. What day of the week is July 4?

3. **Activity** Make a calendar for your favorite month. Be sure to show special days.

1.4.1 Examine the structure of schools and communities in the past.

Going to School

Schools long ago were different from schools today. Look at the picture below. It shows a classroom from long ago. What can you tell from the picture?

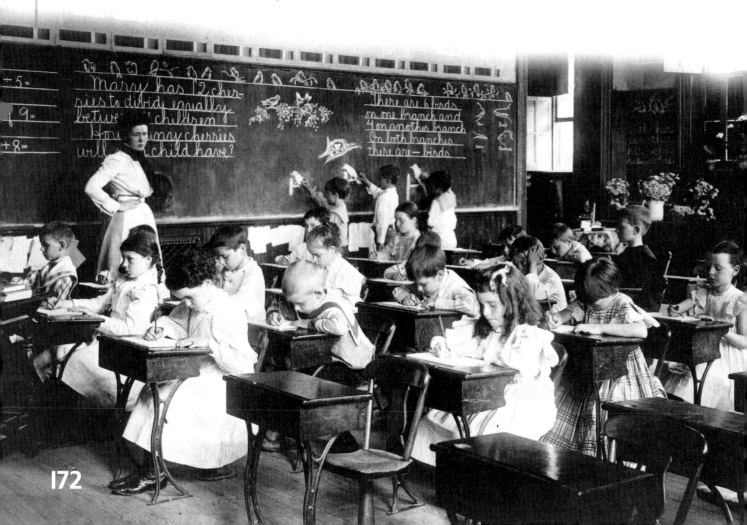

Abacus

Children used different tools to learn. They used an **abacus** to count. An abacus is a frame that holds beads.

Now look at a classroom from today. It has computers. What else do you see?

How is the classroom from the past different from your classroom?

Recess

Many things change with time. One thing that has stayed the same is recess. Recess is a short time when you stop working. Long ago, children went outside at recess.

Long ago, some children played jacks. Others played a game of pickup sticks.

Today, children play games at recess, too. Sometimes they play outside on a playground.

How is recess today the same as it was long ago?

Rules and Manners

There have always been rules in schools. Over time, some of the rules have changed. Some of the rules have stayed the same.

Long ago, children of different ages learned together in the same classroom. They all followed the same rules.

Here is a list of some school
rules from long ago.

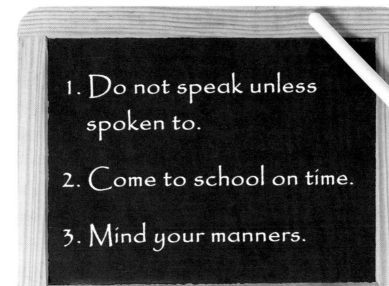

1. Do not speak unless
   spoken to.

2. Come to school on time.

3. Mind your manners.

How are school rules from long ago different from rules today?

Lesson Review

1 What did children use to count long ago?

2 What games were played at recess in the past?

3 **Compare and Contrast** How is school today different from long ago?

Problem Solving

A **problem** is something you need to think about. To **solve** a problem means to find an answer.

To solve a problem,

- Name the problem.
- Think about different ways to fix the problem.
- Choose the best way to solve the problem.

Read the story on the next page about John. Then answer the questions.

John slept late. He may be late for school. What should he do?

Long ago, children walked to school. Today, John can walk to school, too. He can also have an adult drive him to school in a car. It will take John too long to walk. So John asks his mom to drive him to school.

Try the Skill

1 What is John's problem?

2 What are John's choices today to solve the problem?

3 **Activity** Draw a picture showing what you would do.

Maxine Hong Kingston

Maxine Hong Kingston was born on October 27, 1940. She grew up in Stockton, California. Her parents came from China. Her mother loved to tell stories about her family history in China long ago.

Using Primary Sources

"I began writing when I was nine. I was in fourth grade and all of a sudden this poem started coming out of me."

— Maxine Hong Kingston

Maxine loved to hear her mother's stories. Maxine wanted to share stories of her childhood, too. When she grew up, she became a writer.

Many people like to read books by Maxine Hong Kingston.

Why do you think Maxine became a writer?

Maxine meets her readers.

LOG ON

For more about Maxine Hong Kingston, visit:

www.macmillanmh.com/ss/ca/bios

Transportation Then and Now

Transportation is a way of moving people or things from place to place. This took a long time in the past. There were no cars or trains.

In the past, some people walked or rode horses. Others rode in wagons. Trips could take days, weeks, or even months!

People also traveled by boat. It could take a month or more to cross an ocean.

How did people get from place to place long ago?

Trains, Planes, and Cars

People long ago wanted to get to places faster. Some people came up with new ideas, called **inventions**. An invention is something that is made for the first time.

The train was invented. Now people could travel more quickly. Cars were invented, too. Now families could go places more quickly.

Then planes were invented. Planes helped people travel faster than ever.

Look at the chart. It shows how long it takes to travel across our country.

Transportation		Time
wagon		6 months
car		6 days
plane		6 hours

 **Why is transportation faster today?**

Chart and Graph Skills

What kind of transportation is the slowest?

Lesson Review

1. What inventions made traveling faster?

Big Idea 2. How did people get from place to place in the past?

3. **Cause and Effect** Why were trains, cars, and planes invented? What effect did these inventions have on transportation?

Wells Fargo
HISTORY MUSEUM

Welcome to the Wells Fargo History Museum in Los Angeles. Look at the stagecoach. It is from the 1860s.

Now buy your ticket and climb inside. Get ready for a bumpy ride!

People used stagecoaches to travel fast and far. Stagecoaches were also used to deliver the mail.

Los Angeles, California

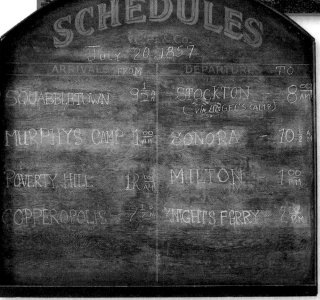

SCHEDULES

JULY 20 1857

ARRIVALS FROM		DEPARTURES TO	
SQUABBLETOWN	9½ A M	STOCKTON (VIA ANGEL'S CAMP)	8⁰⁰ A M
MURPHYS CAMP	1⁰⁰ A M	SONORA	10½ A M
POVERTY HILL	12⁰⁰ A M	MILTON	1⁰⁰ P M
COPPEROPOLIS	7½ P	KNIGHTS FERRY	7⁰⁰ P M

 What was a stagecoach used for?

 For more about Wells Fargo, visit:

www.macmillanmh.com/ss/ca/fieldtrips

Use History Maps

A history map shows how a place looked in the past. Look at the history map on the next page. It shows the trail people took to get from Independence, Missouri to Sacramento, California.

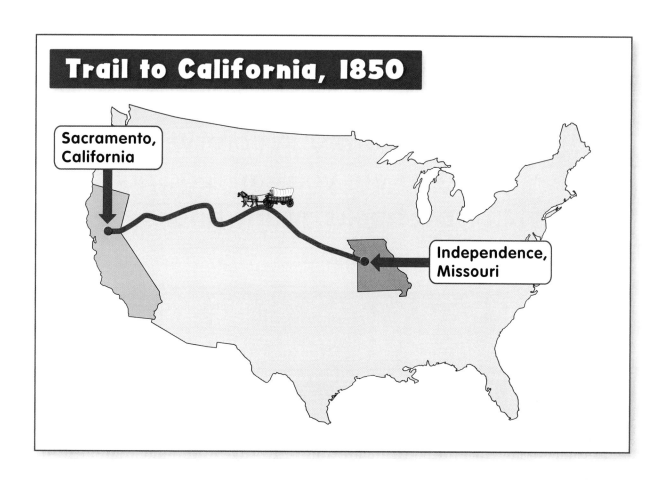

Trail to California, 1850

Sacramento, California

Independence, Missouri

Try the Skill

1. What can a history map show?

2. Where did the trail to California start?

3. **Activity** Suppose you took a trip from Missouri to California. Write a story about the trip.

1.4 Students compare and contrast everyday life in different times and places around the world and recognize that some aspects of people, places, and things change over time while others stay the same.

Discover History

Vocabulary

library

museum

There are many ways to learn about the past. You can visit the **library**. A library is a place where you can read and borrow books. Many books are about history.

You can visit a **museum**, too.
A museum is a place that shows
pictures and things from long ago.
In some museums, you can explore
and touch things from the past.

Lesson Review

1. What can you borrow at a library?

2. **Big Idea** How can a visit to a museum help you learn about the past?

3. **Make Predictions** Suppose you want to read a book about the past. Do you predict you will find it in a museum or in a library?

Helping Kids Have Fun

Spencer Whale lives in Pittsburgh, Pennsylvania. He visited a hospital when he was six years old. He saw that some children in the hospital played with toy cars. The children needed someone to help carry their medicine when they played.

Spencer Whale

Spencer with his invention

Spencer had an idea. He invented a toy car with a special place for the medicine. Now the children could play without the help of someone else.

Spencer said, "It made me very happy that my invention worked. I was happy, too, because the kids have more fun."

Being a Good Citizen

What other inventions help people?

Activity

What could you invent to help others? Draw a picture of it.

Ball Games in
Mexico

Mexico is a country in North America. People in Mexico have always played ball games. One game was called "hip ulama." "Hip ulama" was like soccer. It was played with a rubber ball. One game lasted 8 days! Today, the game is stopped after 2 hours.

A sculpture of a ball player from long ago

A ball court from long ago

Today soccer is a
popular sport in Mexico.
Many people enjoy watching
and playing soccer.

Mexico

A soccer stadium today

Write About It! Write about a ball game played in the United States.

Put Things in Order

Read the paragraph about taking a trip to the museum. Then answer the questions below.

My class visited the transportation museum. First, we walked into the museum. Then, we looked at pictures of transportation from the past. We learned how people traveled long ago. Last, my class rode a bus back to school.

1 What does the class do first in the museum?

2 What does the class do next? What does the class do last?

Vocabulary

3 What is the word for a conversation that you plan?

4 What is an invention?

5 What do we call a place where you can read and borrow books?

Critical Thinking

6 What was school like long ago?

7 How can a visit to the library help you to learn about the past?

Write about It! **8** Name two inventions you have read about. Write about how they changed the way people travel.

Use Calendars

Look at the calendar below. Then use the calendar to answer the questions.

May

Sunday	Monday	Tuesday	Wednesday	Thursday	Friday	Saturday
	1 May Day	2	3	4	5 Cinco de Mayo	6
7	8	9	10	11	12	13
14	15	16	17	18	19	20
21	22	23	24	25	26	27
28	29 Memorial Day	30	31			

1. What is the name of the month on the calendar?

   A   May

   B   July

   C   December

   D   August

2. How many days are in the month of May?

   A   21

   B   31

   C   30

   D   12

3. What holiday is celebrated on May 5?

   A   Mother's Day

   B   Cinco de Mayo

   C   May Day

   D   Thanksgiving

Make a Transportation Invention

1. Draw pictures of transportation from the past and from today.

2. Then think about a transportation invention that you would like to make. Draw a picture of your invention.

3. Write about why people should use your invention.

Read More About the Big Idea

To learn more about history, you can read one of these books.

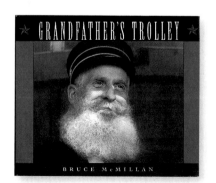

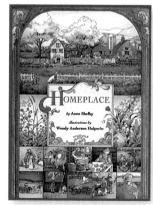

For more about the Big Idea, visit:

www.macmillanmh.com/ss/ca/launchpad

UNIT

5

I.6 Students understand basic economic concepts and the role of individual choice in a free-market economy.

We Work

The Explore Big Idea

Why do people work?

Painter on the
Golden Gate Bridge
in San Francisco

The Big Idea

Explore

Why do people work?

Work is a job that someone does. People work for many reasons. Read about the work that these children do.

"I work at home to help my mom."

"We work hard at school to learn."

"I sell lemonade with my sister. We work to make money!"

In this unit, you will read more about why people work.

An Aesop's Fable

The Ant and the Grasshopper

retold by Noah Michaels

illustrated by Laura Huliska-Beith

Grasshopper loved to have fun. He liked to hop and sing. One day, he saw Ant.

"Come hop and sing with me," said Grasshopper.

Ant said, "I am sorry, but I can not. I have to put food away for winter. You should put food away, too."

Grasshopper said, "I have enough food right now. Why should I worry about winter?"

So Grasshopper hopped and sang all he wanted. Ant kept working.

Winter came. There was no food. Grasshopper was hungry.

Then Grasshopper saw Ant. Ant was eating the corn he had put away in the summer. Now Grasshopper felt hungry and foolish. Grasshopper learned that it is best to work hard and be prepared!

Talk About It! Why did Ant work during the summer?

Vocabulary

About Economics

Read the words in the boxes. Look at the pictures. Learn what the words mean.

Goods are things that are made or grown for people to buy. (page 234)

Services are jobs that people do for others. (page 235)

Work is a job that someone does. (page 202)

Shelter is a place where someone lives. (page 213)

Write About It! What do you see in these pictures?

209

Cause and Effect

Cause and effect show how one thing makes another thing happen.

To find the cause and effect,

- Read the paragraph on the next page. Find out what happens. This is called the effect.

- Read the paragraph again. Look for things that caused the effect.

- Name the cause.
  Name the effect.

You can write the cause and effect in a chart like this.

Cause	Effect

Susan is a gardener. Her job is to take care of flowers. Flowers need water to live. Susan always remembers to water the flowers. She waters the flowers every day. Susan's flowers live and grow.

⋯ Try the Skill ⋯⋯⋯⋯⋯⋯⋯⋯⋯⋯⋯⋯⋯

1. What is the effect of Susan's work?

2. What causes the flowers to live?

3. Explain how you found the cause and effect in the paragraph.

LESSON

1

I.6 Students understand basic economic concepts and the role of individual choice in a free-market economy.

Needs and Wants

Things we must have to live are called **needs**. People need food to eat, water to drink, and clothes to wear.

People also need **shelter**. Shelter is a place where someone lives.

People need love and care, too. Families and friends can help meet these needs.

 **Why do people need food and water?**

Making Choices

Things we would like to have
are called **wants**. We can not have
everything we want. We often
have to make choices.

Juan and his family want a
computer. They also want to
take a trip.

Juan and his family have to choose the computer or the trip. They can not choose both.

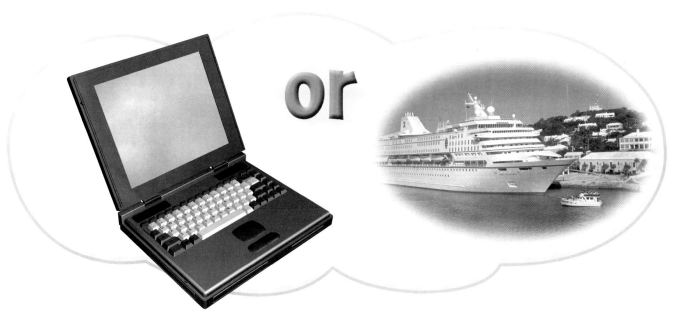

or

 What are wants?

Lesson Review

1. What is the difference between needs and wants?

Big Idea 2. What do people need?

3. **Identify Cause and Effect** Why do people have to make choices?

Use the Internet

The **Internet** is a way for computers to share information. Your computer can get information from a computer on the other side of the world!

Have you ever sent a message to a friend using the Internet? These messages are called e-mails. The e stands for "electronic."

The Internet also has Web sites. A Web site is a group of information in one place.

Look at the Web site below. This Web site tells you about needs and wants. You can find many other Web sites on the Internet.

Try the Skill

1. What is the Internet?

2. Why is the Internet a useful tool?

3. **Activity** Ask your teacher or a parent to help you find a Web site about something that interests you.

LESSON 2

I.6.I Understand the concept of exchange and the use of money to purchase goods and services.

Trade and Money

Vocabulary

trade

money

People sometimes **trade** for things they want or need. You trade when you give one thing to get something else.

What are Mike and Alice trading?

People also use **money** to buy the things they need or want. People get money for work. Money can be coins or paper bills.

Different places in the world have different kinds of money.

U.S. dollars

Pesos from Mexico

Lesson Review

Big Idea

1. What does it mean to trade something?

2. What is one way that people get money?

3. **Compare and Contrast** How are trade and money alike? How are they different?

1.6.1

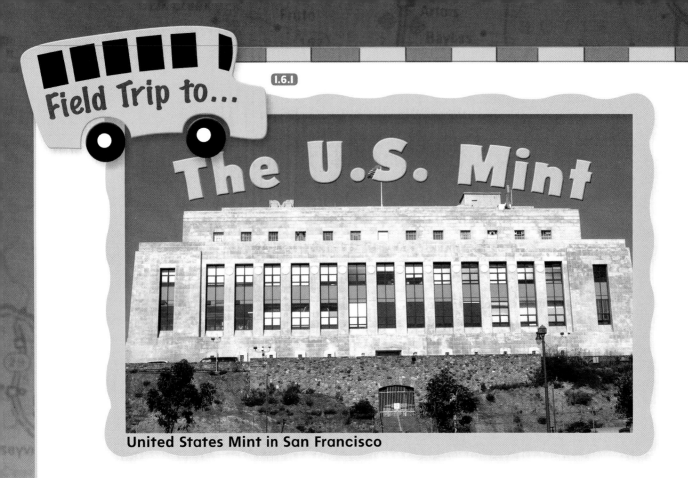

United States Mint in San Francisco

Come along on a visit to the United States Mint in San Francisco. A mint is a place where coins are made. This is how.

1 **First, a machine cuts metal into circles. The circles are called blanks.**

Blanks

2 Next, the blanks are stamped by a coin press.

3 Last, they are checked, placed in coin bags, and sent to banks.

Coin press

California quarter

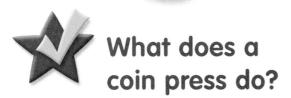

Coin bag

What does a coin press do?

LOG ON For more about the United States Mint, visit:
www.macmillanmh.com/ss/ca/fieldtrips

Use Picture Graphs

A **picture graph** uses pictures to show numbers of things. The title tells you what the picture graph shows.

Sally and Beth sold glasses of lemonade for one quarter each. On which day did they sell the most lemonade? Look at the picture graph on the next page to find out.

The key shows you that one glass stands for one glass of lemonade. Count the glasses next to the word *Friday*. There are three. Sally and Beth sold three glasses of lemonade on Friday.

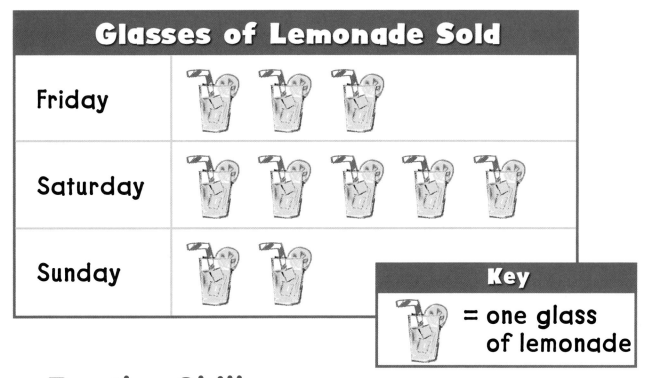

Glasses of Lemonade Sold

Friday	🥤 🥤 🥤
Saturday	🥤 🥤 🥤 🥤 🥤
Sunday	🥤 🥤

Key

🥤 = one glass of lemonade

⋯ Try the Skill ⋯

1 What is the title of the picture graph?

2 On which day did Sally and Beth sell the most lemonade?

3 **Activity** Make a picture graph to show that Sally and Beth sold six glasses of lemonade on Monday.

LESSON

3

I.6.2 Identify the specialized work that people do to manufacture, transport, and market goods and services and the contributions of those who work in the home.

Work and Jobs

Vocabulary

volunteer

People work for many reasons. Most people work at a job to get money.

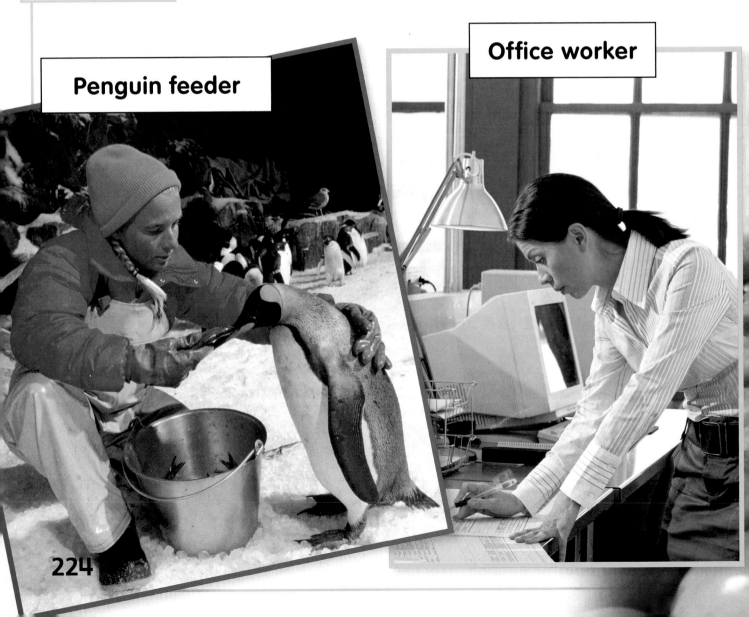

Penguin feeder

Office worker

There are many kinds of jobs. Some people work in an office. They use tools like telephones and computers.

Other people work outdoors. Working hard can be fun!

What do most people get for doing their jobs?

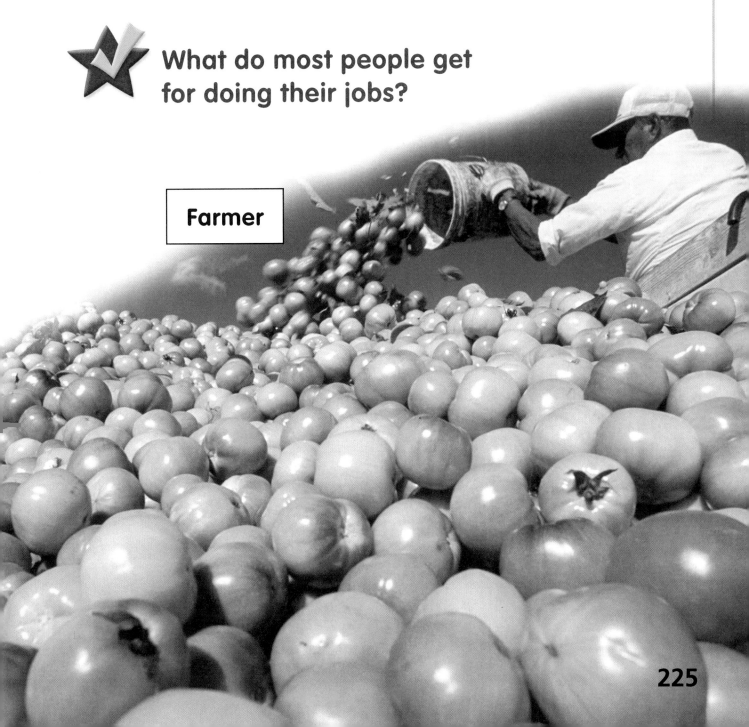

Farmer

The Work We Do

Some people work to help others. A crossing guard helps people to cross the street.

Going to school is one way to prepare to work. A veterinarian is a doctor for animals. Veterinarians must go to school for many years.

Crossing guard

Veterinarian

There are many jobs people can do at home. Some people work at home on a computer.

Many people stay at home to take care of their children.

 What is one way to prepare to work?

Working at home

Working at home

227

We Volunteer

Some people choose to work for free. They are called **volunteers**.

Some volunteers help children to read and write better.

Mrs. Kent is a volunteer. She loves dogs. She walks dogs for an animal shelter.

Look at this picture graph. It shows how many dogs Mrs. Kent walks in three days.

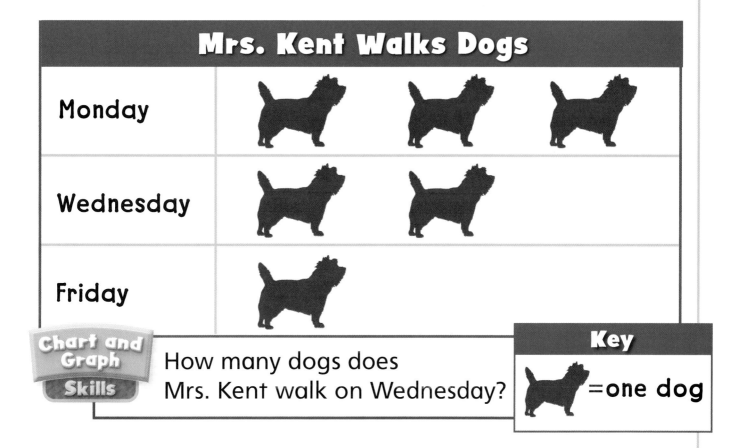

Mrs. Kent Walks Dogs

Monday	🐕 🐕 🐕
Wednesday	🐕 🐕
Friday	🐕

Key

🐕 = one dog

Chart and Graph Skills

How many dogs does Mrs. Kent walk on Wednesday?

Lesson Review

1. Name three places where a person can work.

Big Idea 2. Why might someone choose to volunteer?

3. **Summarize** Tell what this lesson is about in one sentence.

Jimmy Carter

Jimmy Carter was President of the United States from 1977 to 1981. He worked hard to help people.

As a boy, he lived in this farmhouse in Georgia. He loved his home, even though it had no water or electricity!

Jimmy Carter as a boy

After he was President, Jimmy Carter chose to volunteer. He and his wife Rosalynn Carter volunteer to build homes for people. Jimmy Carter believes everyone needs a good home. He is both a leader and a volunteer.

 Why do you think Jimmy Carter volunteers to build homes?

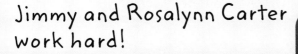
Jimmy and Rosalynn Carter work hard!

LOG ON For more about Jimmy Carter, visit:

www.macmillanmh.com/ss/ca/bios

Celebrate Work with Art

Look at the painting on the next page. It was painted by an artist named Jacob Lawrence.

Jacob Lawrence worked as a painter. He loved to paint and draw as a child. Read what he said.

Using Primary Sources

"Some kids ride bikes, and some kids hike... I liked to color."
—Jacob Lawrence

This painting is called "Builders in the City." When Jacob Lawrence was a boy, he liked to watch carpenters at work.

1.6.2 Identify the specialized work that people do to manufacture, transport, and market goods and services and the contributions of those who work in the home.

Goods and Services

Vocabulary

goods

services

factory

People work to make **goods**. Goods are things that are made or grown for people to buy. Here are some goods.

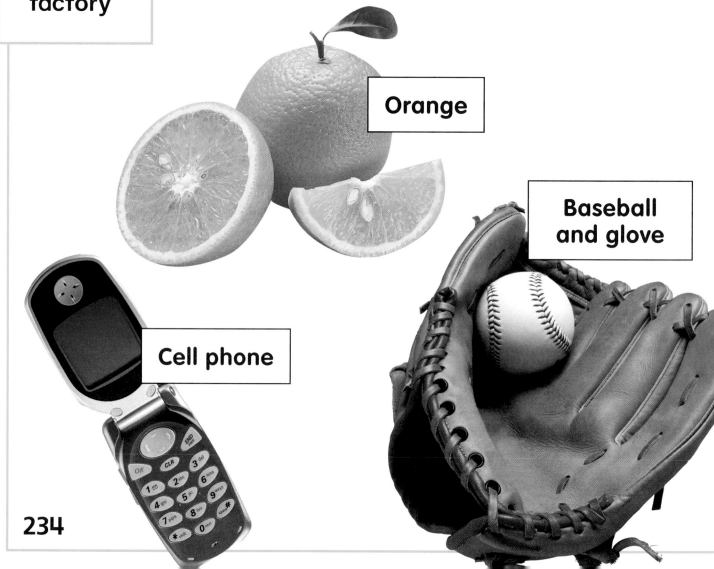

Orange

Baseball and glove

Cell phone

234

Teacher

Dentist

Restaurant server

Services are jobs that people do for others. People are paid for their services. What service jobs are shown above?

 **What is the difference between goods and services?**

From Farmworker to Grocer

Many people work to bring you goods and services. Here are some people who help make and sell orange juice.

Farmworker

The farmworkers pick the oranges from the trees. Then they put the oranges into a truck.

Truck driver

The truck driver takes the oranges from the farm to a building called a **factory**. A factory has machines to make goods.

236

Factory worker

Grocer

Factory workers use machines to squeeze the juice from the oranges. Another machine pours the juice into bottles.

The grocer has a service job. She sells the orange juice to you.

Which of these workers help make goods?

Lesson Review

1 What kind of work is done in a factory?

Big Idea 2 Why does it take many people to help make orange juice?

3 **Put Things in Order** What happens after the farmworkers pick the oranges?

Cooperation and Compromise

Sometimes we do not agree. When this happens, we try to find ways to solve our problem. Cooperation is when people work together.

Here are two apples.

But there are four of us.

238

One way we can work together is to compromise. A compromise is a way we solve a problem. Each person gives something up. Each person also gets something.

I want my own apple.

We can cut them so we can all share.

Citizenship Activity

Tell a story about a time when you made a compromise with a friend.

1.6.2 Identify the specialized work that people do to manufacture, transport, and market goods and services and the contributions of those who work in the home.

Work Long Ago

Long ago, people worked just as they do today.

Many women worked in the home. Some women made clothes. Others taught children how to read and write.

Men also worked. They made goods. Some fixed wagons and coaches.

In the past, many children worked. They needed to make money for their families. Their work was hard. Working children did not have the time to go to school.

Lesson Review

1. What were some jobs women did long ago?

2. Why did some children work long ago?

3. **Identify Cause and Effect** Why were working children unable to go to school?

Jobs in Brazil

People work in every country in the world. Brazil is the biggest country in South America. In Brazil, there are farms, beaches, rain forests, and many large cities. Salvador is a large city in Brazil.

Many people in Brazil farm the land. They grow goods such as cocoa, cotton, corn, and flowers.

Farmer

Salvador

Other people work in service jobs. They work in banks and hotels.

Some people work in factories. Workers make goods such as shoes, cars, and airplanes.

Brazil

Factory worker

Write About It! Write about the kinds of goods people make in Brazil.

Review

John works in a bicycle factory. He makes the metal frame of the bicycle. He also makes the gears and tires. John can make 50 bicycles a day. One day, John stays home from work. The factory does not make as many bicycles that day.

1 What is John's job?

2 What is the effect of John staying home from work one day?

Vocabulary

3 What is work?

4 What is the word for a place where people live?

5 What is a factory?

Critical Thinking

6 How do we get the things we need or want?

7 Why do we need food, clothing, and shelter?

 Write About It! 8 Write why people have to choose between the things they need or want.

Chart and Graph Skills — Use Picture Graphs

1.6.1

Look at the picture graph below. Then use the picture graph to answer the following questions.

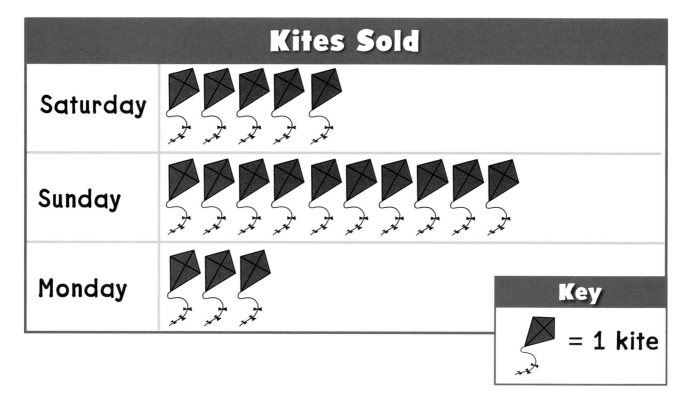

Kites Sold

Saturday	🪁🪁🪁🪁🪁
Sunday	🪁🪁🪁🪁🪁🪁🪁🪁🪁🪁
Monday	🪁🪁🪁

Key
🪁 = 1 kite

1. How many kites were sold on Saturday?

   A 7

   B 5

   C 3

   D 1

2 On which day were three kites sold?

A Friday

B Saturday

C Sunday

D Monday

3 On which day were the most kites sold?

A Friday

B Saturday

C Sunday

D Monday

The Big Idea Activity

My Book of People Working

My Book of People Working

1 Draw pictures of different jobs.

2 Under the pictures, write about each job. Write why someone might like to have the job. Tell if the job provides a service.

3 Make a cover for your book.

4 Share your book with your class.

Read More About the Big Idea

To learn more about work and money, you can read one of these books.

LAUNCH PAD

For help with the Big Idea activity, visit:

www.macmillanmh.com/ss/ca/launchpad

UNIT

6

I.5 Students describe the human characteristics of familiar places and the varied backgrounds of American citizens and residents in those places.

All Together

The Big Idea

Explore

How are we alike and different?

We come from many places.

How are we alike and different?

Vocabulary

culture

Americans come from all around the world. Different people have different **cultures**. Culture is the way a group of people live.

"We may eat different foods."

"We may celebrate
different holidays."

"We all have friends
and families."

In this unit, you will read
more about how we are alike
and different.

Literature

A World of Cultures

written by Juan Gonzalez
illustrated by Chi Chung

We share this world together.

We live in different ways.

We sing and dance and celebrate
  on special holidays.

Our customs may be different,
  our language and music, too.
But the need for clothing, food, and love
  are the same for me and you!

Talk About It!

In what ways are all people the same?

253

Vocabulary
About Culture

Read the words in the boxes. Then look at the pictures. Learn what the words mean.

Moccasins are a soft kind of shoe. (page 267)

A **tradition** is a way of doing something that is passed down over time.

(page 282)

An **immigrant** is a person who moves to a new country. (page 270)

(page 270)

Write About It!

What do you see in these pictures?

255

Social
Studies

Compare and Contrast

When we **compare** two things, we find out how they are the same. When we **contrast** two things, we find out how they are different.

To compare and contrast,

- Read the paragraphs.
- Find one thing that is the same.
- Find one thing that is different.

Put your information in a Venn diagram like the one below.

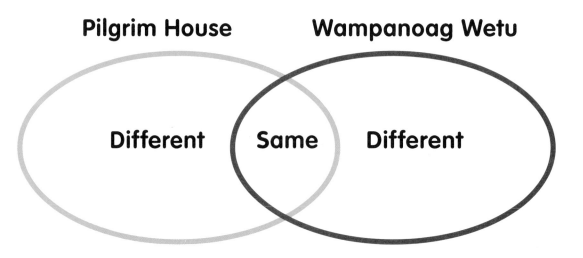

Pilgrim House　　**Wampanoag Wetu**

Different　　**Same**　　**Different**

Read the paragraphs about Pilgrim and Wampanoag homes. Then try the skill.

Pilgrim house

The Pilgrims lived in wooden houses. Their houses were small. The roof was made with straw.

The Wampanoag lived in small houses called wetu. A wetu was made of grass and wooden poles.

Wampanoag wetu

Try the Skill

1 Compare the Wampanoag wetu and Pilgrim house. Find one way they are alike.

2 Contrast the Wampanoag wetu and Pilgrim house. Find one way they are different.

3 Which type of home do you like best and why?

1.5 Students describe the human characteristics of familiar places and the varied backgrounds of American citizens and residents in those places.

1.5.3 Compare the beliefs, customs, ceremonies, traditions, and social practices of the varied cultures, drawing from folklore.

A Trip Around the World

Vocabulary

custom

People live all over the world. People in different places have different **customs**. A custom is a special way a group does something.

In Puerto Rico, people celebrate by having a fiesta. They dance to lively music. The dancers twirl, spin, and clap their hands.

Puerto Rico

258

In Russia, music and dance are important, too. Some dances start out slowly. Then the music gets faster. Dancers stamp their feet or bend their knees and kick.

Russia

What are two ways people celebrate?

The World in Our School

Some children in your class may be new to this country. You can learn about their customs.

Meet Juan. He is from Mexico. It is his custom to say "Hola!" when he greets a friend.

Meet Julia. She is from Poland. It is her custom to dance the polka at a celebration.

Meet Soo Jin. She is from South Korea. It is her custom to bow when she greets an adult.

Meet Jasmine. She is from California. It is her custom to say "Have a nice day!" to people she greets.

 **What are two customs from around the world?**

Lesson Review

1. Name one custom from the United States.

Big Idea 2. Tell about a custom that you follow in your home or community.

3. **Compare and Contrast** Compare and contrast the way people celebrate in Russia and Puerto Rico.

Sort into Groups

Look at the picture. You can **sort** the shoes you see in different ways. To sort means to put things that are alike into a group. All of these items are shoes. You could name this group "Shoes."

Look at the two groups below. How are the shoes in each group alike?

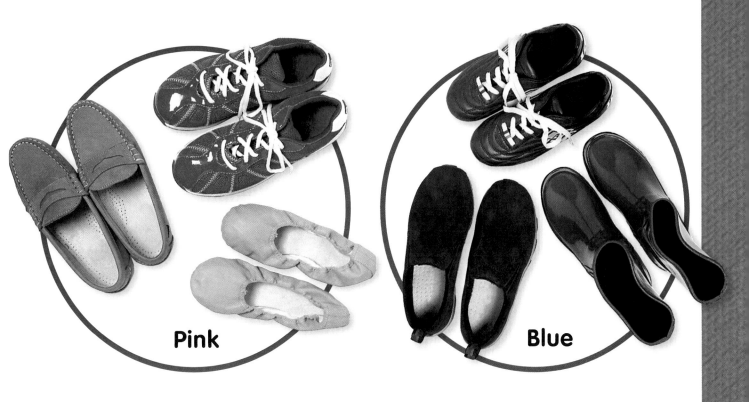

Pink

Blue

Try the Skill

1. Sort the shoes with laces into one group. Put the shoes without laces in another group. How many pairs of shoes have laces?

2. What is another way you can sort the shoes?

3. **Activity** Draw a picture of your favorite fruits and vegetables. Find two ways to sort them.

I.5.2 Understand the ways in which American Indians and immigrants have helped define Californian and American culture.

The First Americans

Vocabulary

canoe

moccasin

Native Americans, or American Indians, were the first people to live in North America. They have lived here for more than ten thousand years!

There are many Native American groups. Each group is different. Each group has its own culture.

Who were the first people to live in North America?

Gifts from Native Americans

Native Americans have made many wonderful things. They made a type of boat called a **canoe**. A canoe is a thin boat that can move fast.

They made a great snack from corn. Popcorn!

Canoe

Long ago nearly all Native Americans wore **moccasins**. Moccasins are a soft kind of shoe. Each group decorated its moccasins in its own way. You could tell a person's group by looking at their moccasins!

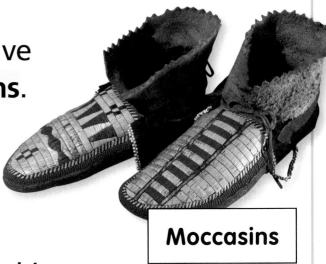

Moccasins

 **What are some things that Native Americans have made?**

Lesson Review

1. How long have Native Americans lived in North America?

Big Idea 2. How can moccasins help you learn about a Native American person?

3. **Summarize:** Tell what you have learned about Native Americans.

Sequoyah

Sequoyah was a Cherokee Indian. Long ago, the Cherokee did not have a written language. Sequoyah decided to invent one!

He made an alphabet. It was made up of 85 symbols.

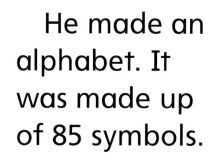

Now all Cherokee children could learn to read and write their language. Soon the Cherokee had their own books and newspapers.

 How did Sequoyah help all the Cherokee?

 For more about Sequoyah, visit: www.macmillanmh.com/ss/ca/bios

LESSON

I.5.2 Understand the ways in which American Indians and immigrants have helped define Californian and American culture.

People Come to America

Vocabulary

immigrant

Native Americans lived in North America for a long time. Then **immigrants** began to come to the continent. An immigrant is a person who moves to a new country.

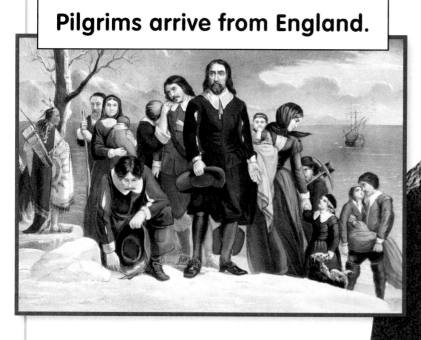

Pilgrims arrive from England.

Spanish immigrants arrive from Mexico.

The United States is a country of immigrants. For many years, immigrants have come from all over the world.

Immigrants come to the United States for many reasons. Many come for freedom. Some come for jobs. Others come to be with their families. All immigrants come for a better life.

 Why do immigrants come to the United States to live?

Immigrants see the Statue of Liberty in New York harbor.

Gifts from Immigrants

Immigrants bring their customs to the United States. They bring their languages, foods, and sports.

Over time, immigrant customs become American customs. The hot dog is one example. It came from German immigrants who liked to eat sausages with mustard. Today the hot dog is a popular American food.

Immigrants also bring their sports to the United States. English immigrants brought a game called rounders.

Over time, rounders became the American game, baseball. Today baseball is a popular American sport.

What do immigrants bring to the United States?

Lesson Review

1. Name a custom from another country.

 2. How is our country's culture special?

3. **Cause and Effect** What is one cause for an immigrant to move to the United States? What might be the effect?

I.5.2

Immigrant Children in the 1930s

Meet Josephine and John. Their family came to the United States from Italy. They live in a small apartment at 97 Orchard Street in New York City.

We share meals and stories in our cozy kitchen. ▼

We have many neighbors in our apartment building. We like the baby who lives upstairs. ▶

"In front of our house, at the stoop, we play hopscotch and kick the can."
—Josephine Baldizzi

◀ We play marbles, too.

We love to hear stories on the radio. ▶

Write About It!

Write a story about a day in the life of Josephine or John.

LOG ON
For more about life in the 1930s, visit our Web site at:
www.macmillanmh.com/ss/ca/dayinthelife

1.5.2

A New Kid on the Block

Characters

Maria,
from
Puerto Rico

Ira,
from
Russia

Joe,
from
Ireland

Anna,
from
Poland

- Shoemaker

Narrator: In the 1920s, many immigrants arrived in New York City. They came from all over the world. Many immigrant children did not go to school. Instead they worked. Sometimes they found time to play.

Shoemaker: Maria, I am going out for a little while. Please fix these shoes.

Maria: Yes, ma'am.

(The shoemaker walks away.)

Maria: Who wants to play a game of stickball?

Ira: I will play!

(Ira puts down his newspapers.)

Maria: How about you, Joe?

Joe: I want to, but I have to work. I have chestnuts to sell.

Maria: You can sell them later. Come on! We have me, you, and Ira. That's three.

Joe: That's not enough. We need one more kid. Who can we find?

(Anna walks in front of them. She is carrying a suitcase. She looks lost.)

Ira: Hey, what about her?

Maria: Great idea! Hey, kid!

Anna: Hello.

Ira: Do you want to play stickball?

Anna: I do not speak much English.

Joe: What country are you from?

Anna: Poland. I just came from the boat.

(Anna starts to cry.)

Ira: Do not worry. We all came here from other places.

Joe: That is true. I came from Ireland. Ira is from Russia.

Maria: And I came from Puerto Rico. Where is your family?

Anna: My aunt was to meet me at the boat. But she was not there. Now I am lost.

(Suddenly, the shoemaker runs in.)

Shoemaker: Anna, is that you?

Anna: Aunt Eva!

Shoemaker: I could not find you on the boat.

Anna: I could not find you either!

Shoemaker: Maria, what are you doing? You should be watching the shop.

Anna: Do not be angry, Aunt Eva. These kids wanted to show me an American game.

Shoemaker: I will let you play just this once. Then it is back to work!

Maria, Ira, Joe: Hurray! Let us play!

Maria: You are going to love it in America. You will see!

Narrator: The end.

Write About It! What do you think happens next in Anna's story?

Use Time Lines

A **time line** is a line that shows the order of when things happen. Look at Julia's time line below.

Julia's Time Line

2000

2002

A baby picture of me.
I was one month old.

A holiday celebration.
I was two years old.

Point to the first picture on the time line. It shows Julia when she was a baby.

Try the Skill

1. What does a time line show?

2. What happened when Julia was four?

3. **Activity** Make a time line about your life.

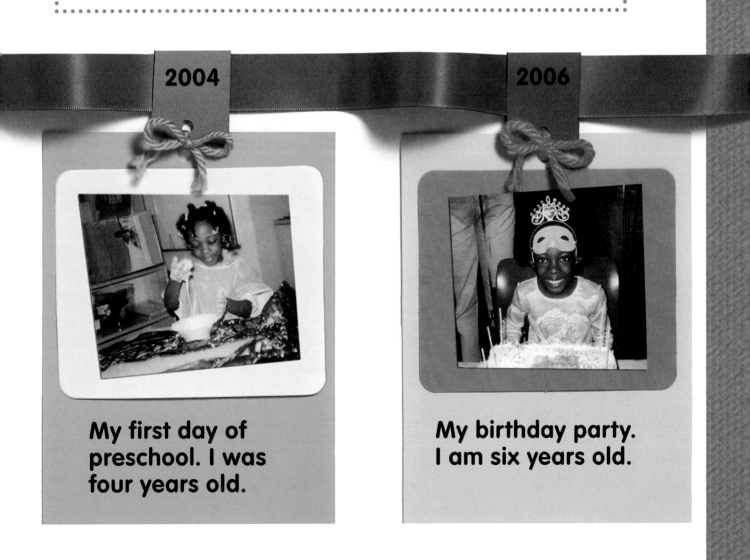

2004

My first day of preschool. I was four years old.

2006

My birthday party. I am six years old.

I.5.I Recognize the ways in which they are all part of the same community, sharing principles, goals, and traditions despite their varied ancestry; the forms of diversity in their school and community; and the benefits and challenges of a diverse population.

Traditions We Share

Vocabulary

tradition

A **tradition** is a way of doing something that is passed down over time. In the United States we have many traditions. We celebrate Thanksgiving with a feast. We say the Pledge of Allegiance to our flag.

American traditions help us feel like we are a part of a group. Families, friends, and neighbors join together to celebrate.

What are some of our traditions?

We Respect One Another

American citizens come from many different cultures. We respect our different ways.

We learn new ways to do things. We eat food that we never tasted before.

We learn new traditions from our friends. We are proud of our many cultures.

 How can we show respect to our classmates?

Lesson Review

1 What traditions do all Americans share?

Big Idea

2 Why is it important to show respect to everyone's culture?

3 **Compare and Contrast** Make a list of your family traditions. Share it with a classmate. Find the ways in which you and your classmates are the same and different.

Primary Sources 1.5

Use Artifacts

An artifact is an old object that tells us something about the past. The poster on the next page is an artifact.

Look Closely

Look at the poster. It told people about a new form of transportation, the train. The poster said that the train could go across the continent fast.

ACROSS THE CONTINENT

Once 32 days
Now 4 days

THE FARGO WAY

Primary Source Review

1 How long does the poster say it will take the train to go across the continent?

2 What other form of transportation do you see on the poster?

3 Do you think the poster made people want to take a train? Why?

Getting Along at School

Ms. Cater teaches first grade in Oakland, California. In Ms. Cater's class, everyone learns special rules for getting along. One rule is no put-downs. Carlos Reyes says, "This means no calling people names."

Another rule is to talk it out. Dalia Jasso says, "We try to talk instead of fight. If someone pushes me on the playground, I don't push back. I say I don't like when you push me."

Dalia and Carlos want to help others get along.

Oakland, California

Carlos Alfredo Reyes

Dalia Jasso Silva

Being a Good Citizen ★ ★ ★

What rules help you get along with other people in your school?

Activity

Suppose that someone is calling you a name you do not like. What should you do?

289

The First People of Australia

Australia is a continent and a country. The first people who lived there are called the First People.

Traditions are important to them. One tradition is telling stories about nature. They tell many of their stories by singing them.

Art is an important tradition, too. Sand painting and bark painting are two kinds of traditional art.

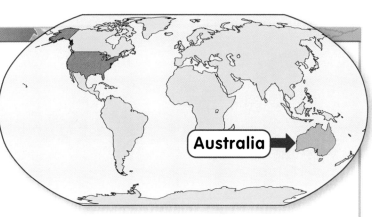

Australia

Bark painting

Write About It! What traditions are important to the First People of Australia?

Reading Social Studies **Compare and Contrast**

Read the paragraphs. Then answer the questions.

Igloo

People have different kinds of houses. In Alaska, some people live in igloos.

In the desert in Africa, some people live in houses made of clay.

Clay house

1 Compare and contrast an igloo and a clay house. How are they different? How are they the same?

2 How is your home like an igloo? How is it different?

Vocabulary

3 What do you call a special way a group does something?

4 What is an immigrant?

5 What does the word "culture" mean?

Critical Thinking

6 Why are traditions important?

7 What are customs that you follow at home and in school?

 8 Write about what immigrants bring to a new country.

Chart and Graph Skills — **Use Time Lines**

The time line shows when Juan, Julia, and Soo Jin moved to California. Use the time line to answer the following questions.

2002

Juan moves to California.

1 What year did Soo Jin move to California?

    A   2002

    B   2006

    C   2004

    D   2003

2 Who moved to California in 2004?

    A   Julia

    B   Soo Jin

    C   Juan

    D   Jasmine

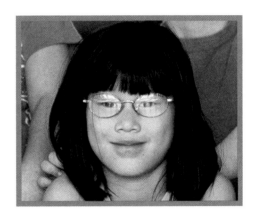

2004

2006

Julia moves to California.

Soo Jin moves to California.

3 Who moved to California first?

A Soo Jin

B Julia

C Juan

D Paul

The Big Idea Activity

Make an Accordion Book of Customs and Traditions

1. Fold a large sheet of paper like the one in the picture.

2. Draw pictures that show different customs and traditions.

3. Write a sentence about each one.

Read More About the Big Idea

To learn more about culture, you can read one of these books.

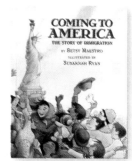

For help with the Big Idea activity, visit:

www.macmillanmh.com/ss/ca/launchpad

296

Reference Section Contents

Holidays

Celebrate Holidays

We celebrate many holidays. Holidays are days when we celebrate special people and events. They are times to celebrate our families and communities.

Veterans' Day

On Veterans' Day, we celebrate veterans. A veteran is a person who has protected our country. A veteran is a hero.

Activity

Make a "Celebrate Veterans" Flag
- Ask your family and friends for the names of veterans.
- Write each name on a star.
- Paste them on a flag.

Thanksgiving

The Pilgrims came to North America long ago. The Native Americans showed the Pilgrims how to fish, farm, and hunt. The Pilgrims gave thanks by sharing a meal with their friends.

We celebrate Thanksgiving every year. We share a special meal with friends and family.

Activity

Make a Collage

- Draw pictures of things you are thankful for.
- Paste your pictures on a paper plate turkey.

On Christmas, Christians celebrate the birth of Jesus. Many Christians put stars on top of Christmas trees. They also give gifts.

Jewish people celebrate Hanukkah. They light candles for eight days. They put the candles in a special candleholder called a "menorah." Hanukkah is also called the Festival of Lights.

Some African Americans celebrate Kwanzaa. Kwanzaa takes place from December 26 to January I. On these days, people share food and remember their past.

Muslims celebrate Eid al-Fitr. Eid al-Fitr is the last day of a month called Ramadan. During Ramadan, Muslims think about their lives. On Eid al-Fitr, Muslims celebrate by giving gifts to help others.

Activity

Make a Holiday Cookbook
- **Draw pictures of food from different holidays.**
- **Make the pictures into a book.**

Martin Luther King, Jr., Day

We celebrate Martin Luther King, Jr., Day in January. Martin Luther King, Jr., worked hard to make our laws fair. On this day, we remember how Martin Luther King, Jr., made America a better place.

Activity

Make a Friendship Circle

- Trace the hand of a classmate.
- Cut out the shape.
- Write a sentence about being friends.
- Paste the hands in a big circle.
- Paste the sentences inside the circle.

Friendship Circle

Any person can be a friend.

Let's all be friends

People should work together.

Be nice to your neighbor.

Be Kind to all people.

Presidents' Day

In February, we celebrate Presidents' Day. This special day helps us to remember Presidents George Washington and Abraham Lincoln.

Activity

Make coin rubbings of George Washington and Abraham Lincoln

- **Cover quarters and pennies with white paper.**
- **Rub a crayon over the paper.**
- **Decorate with your own drawings.**

Cesar Chavez Day

Cesar Chavez was a hero to many. He worked hard to help workers in his community. He made sure they were paid fairly for their hard work. On Cesar Chavez Day, we think of ways that we can help our communities.

Activity

Make a Picture

- Think of a way you can help your community.
- Draw a picture of how you can help.

Cinco de Mayo

Cinco de Mayo means the "fifth of May" in Spanish. It celebrates the day that Mexico won a battle against France. Today, Mexicans and Mexican Americans celebrate with parties and parades.

Activity

Make a Poncho

- Cut a hole in a paper bag for your head.
- Cut a slit on each side for your arms.
- Paint designs on the bag.
- Add bits of yarn with glue.

Flag Day

We celebrate Flag Day on June 14. On that day long ago, our country chose its first flag. Today, our flag has fifty stars that stand for the fifty states in our country. To celebrate Flag Day, we fly the American flag.

Activity

Make a Card

- Fold a sheet of paper in half.
- Draw a picture of our flag on the outside.
- Write a Flag Day message on the inside.

Independence Day

Independence Day celebrates the birthday of the United States of America. It is also called the Fourth of July. We celebrate with parades. We also watch fireworks.

Activity

Make a Fireworks Painting

- Use a black piece of paper.
- Make glue designs.
- Sprinkle with glitter.

ARCTIC OCEAN

RUSSIA

CANADA

ALASKA

Juneau

PACIFIC OCEAN

CANADA

★Olympia
WASHINGTON

MONTANA
★Helena

★Salem

OREGON

IDAHO
★Boise

WYOMING

Cheyenne★

WEST

Carson
City

Salt Lake★
City

Denver ★

Sacramento ★

NEVADA

UTAH

COLORADO

CALIFORNIA

PACIFIC
OCEAN

ARIZONA

Santa Fe★

NEW
MEXICO

★Phoenix

MEXICO

HAWAII
Honolulu★

PACIFIC OCEAN

Map Key

⊛ National capital
★ State capital

NORTH

CANADA

NORTH DAKOTA
★ Bismarck

MINNESOTA

Lake Superior

SOUTH DAKOTA
★ Pierre

St. Paul ★

WISCONSIN

MICHIGAN

Lake Huron

Lake Michigan

Lake Ontario

NEW HAMPSHIRE
VERMONT

MAINE
★ Augusta

Montpelier ★

★ Concord
★ Boston

Albany ★

NEW YORK

MASSACHUSETTS

★ Providence

Hartford

RHODE ISLAND
CONNECTICUT

Madison ★

Lansing ★

Lake Erie

PENNSYLVANIA

Trenton ★

NEBRASKA

IOWA
★ Des Moines

ILLINOIS

INDIANA

Columbus ★

OHIO

Harrisburg ★

NEW JERSEY

Lincoln ★

Dover ★

DELAWARE

Washington, D.C. ✪

Annapolis

Springfield ★

Indianapolis ★

WEST VIRGINIA

MARYLAND

Topeka ★

Jefferson City ★

★ Frankfort

★ Charleston

★ Richmond

KANSAS

MISSOURI

KENTUCKY

VIRGINIA

EAST

Nashville ★

★ Raleigh

Oklahoma City
★

ARKANSAS

TENNESSEE

NORTH CAROLINA

OKLAHOMA

Little Rock ★

Columbia ★

SOUTH CAROLINA

Atlanta ★

TEXAS

ALABAMA

GEORGIA

ATLANTIC OCEAN

MISSISSIPPI
★ Jackson

Montgomery ★

LOUISIANA

★ Tallahassee

Baton Rouge ★

Austin ★

FLORIDA

Gulf of Mexico

THE BAHAMAS

SOUTH

CUBA

THE UNITED STATES AND ITS NEIGHBORS

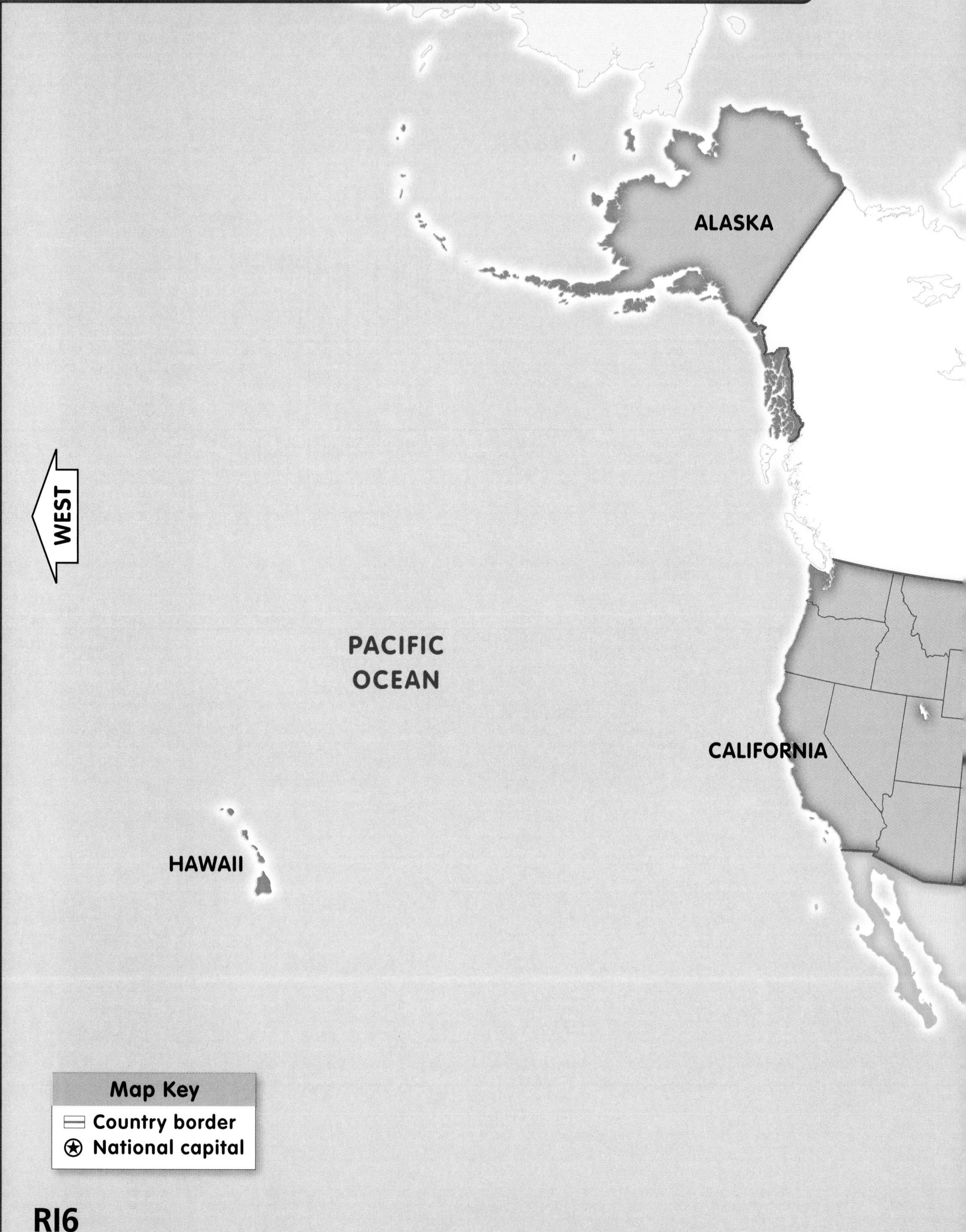
ALASKA
WEST
PACIFIC
OCEAN
CALIFORNIA
HAWAII
Map Key
Country border
National capital

NORTH

EAST

CANADA

Ottawa ✪

UNITED STATES

Washington, D.C. ✪

ATLANTIC
OCEAN

MEXICO

✪ Mexico City

SOUTH

R17

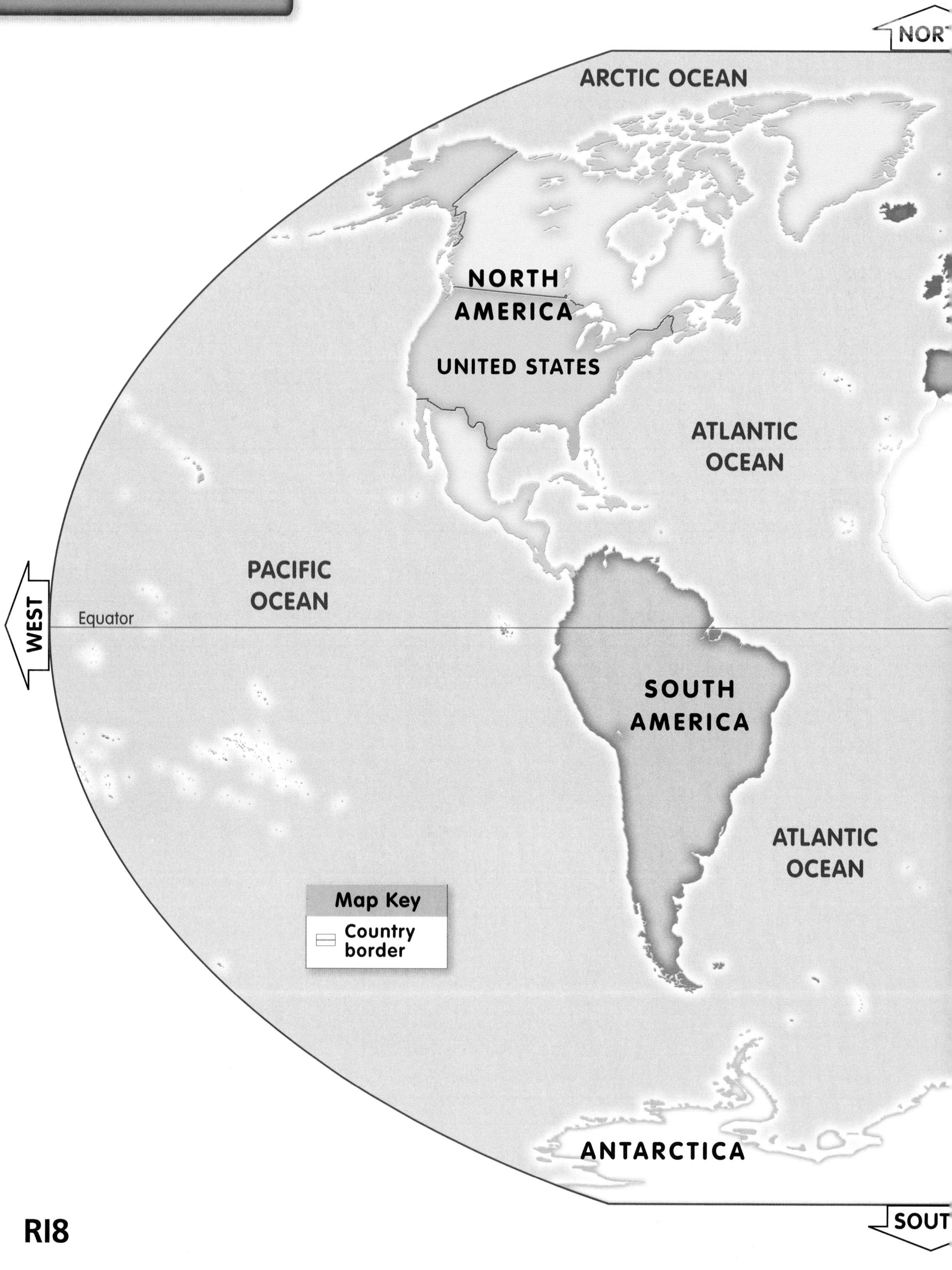

NOR

ARCTIC OCEAN

NORTH
AMERICA

UNITED STATES

ATLANTIC
OCEAN

PACIFIC
OCEAN

WEST

Equator

SOUTH
AMERICA

ATLANTIC
OCEAN

Map Key

Country
border

ANTARCTICA

SOUT

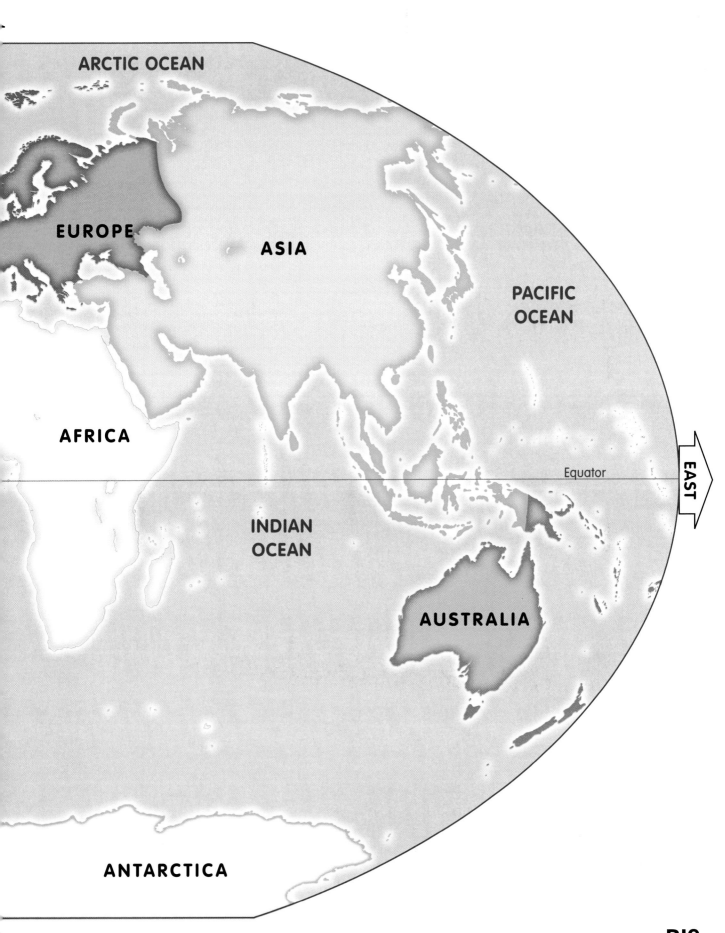

ARCTIC OCEAN

EUROPE

ASIA

PACIFIC
OCEAN

AFRICA

Equator

EAST

INDIAN
OCEAN

AUSTRALIA

ANTARCTICA

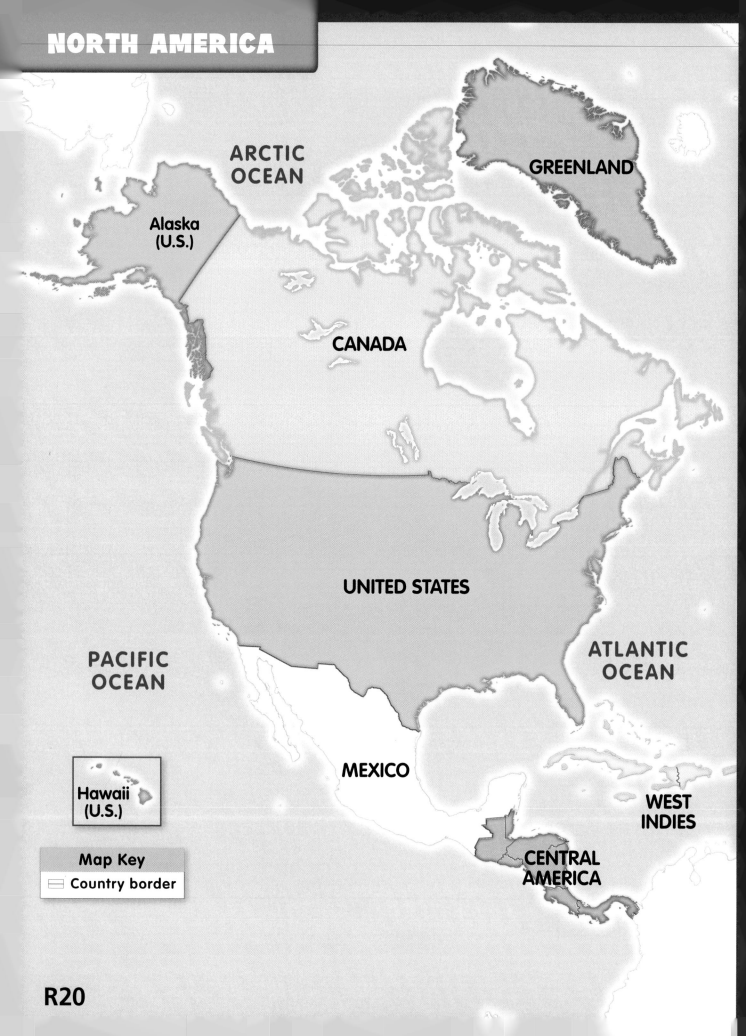

ARCTIC
OCEAN

GREENLAND

Alaska
(U.S.)

CANADA

UNITED STATES

PACIFIC
OCEAN

ATLANTIC
OCEAN

MEXICO

Hawaii
(U.S.)

WEST
INDIES

Map Key
Country border

CENTRAL
AMERICA

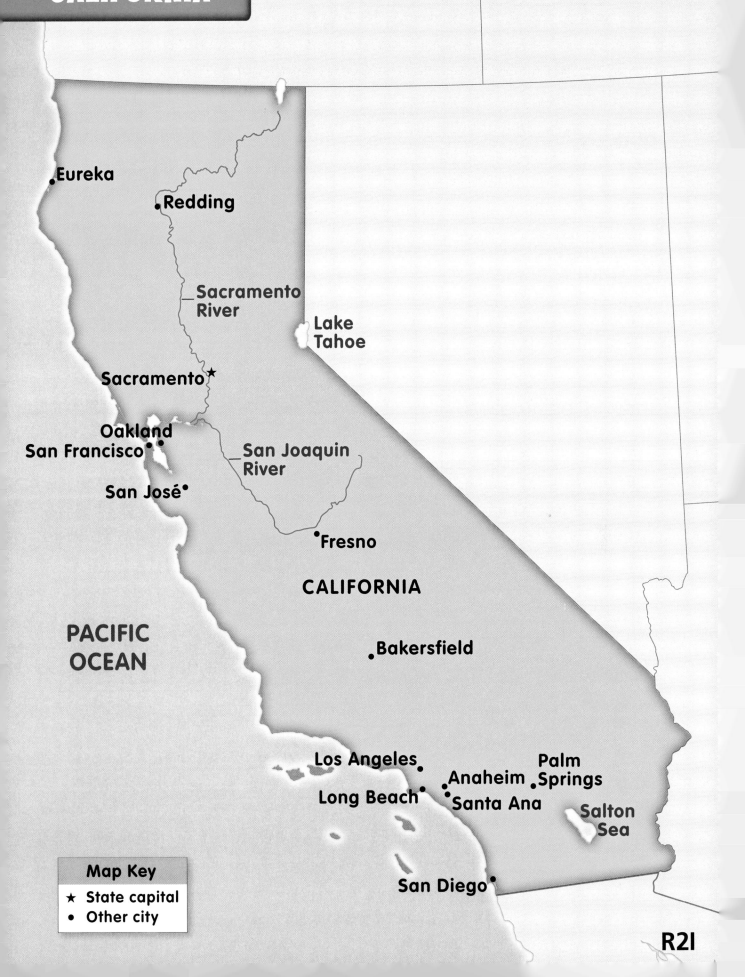

CALIFORNIA

Eureka

Redding

Sacramento River

Lake Tahoe

Sacramento ★

Oakland
San Francisco

San José

San Joaquin River

Fresno

CALIFORNIA

PACIFIC OCEAN

Bakersfield

Los Angeles

Palm Springs

Anaheim

Long Beach

Santa Ana

Salton Sea

San Diego

Map Key
★ State capital
• Other city

R21

Picture Glossary

A

abacus An **abacus** is a frame with beads used for counting. (page 173)

absolute location An **absolute location** tells the exact spot where a place is. (page 14)

address An **address** is a way to find places. (page 14)

C

calendar A **calendar** is a chart that shows the months, weeks, and days of a year. (page 170)

canoe A **canoe** is a thin boat that can move fast. (page 266)

celebrate To **celebrate** is to do something special. (page 106)

chart **Charts** use words and pictures to show things. (page 72)

citizen A **citizen** is a person who belongs to a country. (page 58)

city A **city** is a big and busy place where many people live. (page 18)

community A **community** is a group of people who live in the same neighborhood. (page 76)

compare To **compare** means to find out how things are alike. (page 256)

continent A **continent** is a large body of land. (page 30)

contrast To **contrast** means to find out how things are different. (page 256)

country A **country** is a land and the people who live there. (page 28)

culture **Culture** is the way a group of people live. (page 250)

custom A **custom** is a special way a group does something. (page 258)

D

diagram A **diagram** shows the different parts of something. (page 134)

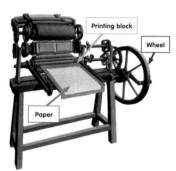

Printing block

Wheel

Paper

directions **Directions** tell us which way to go. (page 78)

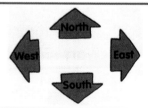

North

West

East

South

document A **document** is a piece of paper with writing on it. (page 132)

E

Earth The planet we live on is **Earth**. (page 26)

F

factory A **factory** is a place where machines make goods. (page 236)

feast A **feast** is a large meal. (page 123)

flag A **flag** is a symbol of a country. (page 114)

G

geography **Geography** is the study of places. (page 2)

globe A **globe** is a model of Earth. (page 26)

goods **Goods** are things that are made or grown for people to buy. (page 234)

government A **government** is a group of people who work for all the citizens of a country. (page 143)

group A **group** is made up of many people. (page 66)

H

history **History** is what happened in the past. (page 154)

history map A **history map** shows how a place looked in the past. (page 188)

holiday A **holiday** is a special day. (page 124)

I

immigrant An **immigrant** is a person who moves to a new country. (page 270)

independence **Independence** means freedom. (page 128)

Internet The **Internet** is a way for computers to share information. (page 216)

interview An **interview** is a conversation that you plan. (page 166)

invention An **invention** is something that is made for the first time. (page 184)

law A **law** is a rule we must follow in our community. (page 76)

leader A **leader** is the head of a group. (page 84)

library A **library** is a place where you can read and borrow books. (page 190)

M

main idea The **main idea** tells what a story is about. (page 10)

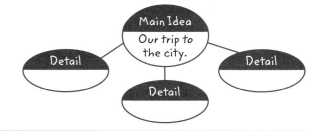

map key A **map key** tells what the symbols on a map mean. (page 16)

mayor A **mayor** is the leader of a community. (page 90)

moccasins Moccasins are a soft kind of shoe. (page 254)

model A **model** is a small copy of a place or object. (page 26)

money Money is what people use to buy things they need or want. (page 219)

monument A **monument** is a building or statue that helps us to remember the past. (page 136)

museum A **museum** is a building that shows pictures and things from the past. (page 191)

N

Native Americans Native Americans were the first people to live in America. (page 123)

needs Needs are things we must have to live. (page 212)

neighborhood A **neigborhood** is a place where people live. (page 12)

O

ocean An **ocean** is a very large body of water. (page 32)

P

picture graph A **picture graph** uses pictures to show numbers of things. (page 222)

prediction A **prediction** is a guess about what will happen next. (page 64)

What I Know	What I Predict

primary source A **primary source** is a thing from the past that helps us learn. (page 86)

problem A **problem** is something you need to think about. (page 178)

R

relative location **Relative location** tells what something is near. The phone is near the computer. (page 20)

respect **Respect** is concern for others. (page 68)

responsibility A **responsibility** is a thing we must do. (page 95)

right A **right** is a thing we are free to do. (page 94)

rule **Rules** tell us what to do. (page 74)

S

seasons **Seasons** are the four parts of the year. The seasons are spring, summer, fall, and winter. (page 42)

services **Services** are jobs that people do for others. (page 235)

shelter **Shelter** is a place where someone lives. (page 213)

solve To **solve** a problem means to find an answer. (page 178)

sort To **sort** means to put things that are alike into a group. (page 262)

state A **state** is part of a country. (page 28)

suburb A **suburb** is a quiet place near the city where people live. (page 19)

summarize To **summarize** is to say what a paragraph is about in one sentence. (page 112)

Summary
This paragraph is about a day at the beach.

symbol A **symbol** is something that stands for something else. (page 114)

T

time line A **time line** is a line that shows the order of when things happen. (page 280)

town A **town** is a place far from a city where people live. (page 19)

trade To **trade** is to give one thing to get something else. (page 218)

tradition A **tradition** is something that is passed down over time. (page 282)

transportation **Transportation** is a way of moving people and things from place to place. (page 182)

V

volunteers **Volunteers** are people who choose to work for free. (page 228)

vote A **vote** is a choice that can be counted. (page 82)

W

wants **Wants** are things we would like to have. (page 214)

weather Weather is what the air is like outside. (page 40)

work Work is a job that someone does. (page 202)

Index

This index is a list of things you can find in your book. It tells you the page numbers on which they are found. Sometimes you will see the letter *m* in front of the page number. The letter *m* tells you a map is on that page.

CREDITS

Photography Credits: All photographs are by Macmillan/McGraw-Hill School Division (MMH) and Ken Karp for MMH, except as noted below:

COVER PHOTOS: Front Cover: (t) D. Falconer/PhotoLink/Photodisc/Getty Images; (b) ©Tom & Dee Ann McCarthy/CORBIS. Back Cover: (bkgd) ©M. Angelo/CORBIS; (inset) Arthur Tilley/Creatas/PictureQuest. Endpapers: (flag) Macmillan/McGraw-Hill; (seal) One Mile Up/Fotosearch, LLC. iii: ©Craig Hammell/CORBIS. iv: Lawrence Migdale PIX. vi: ©Charles E. Rotkin/CORBIS. vii: (l) ©Frances Benjamin Johnston/CORBIS; (r) ©Ellen Senisi/The Image Works . viii: Taxi/Getty Images. ix: Ariel Skelley/Masterfile. xiii: The Granger Collection, New York. G2-G3: (bkgd) Todd Bannor/Alamy. G3: Courtesy of Steve Cunha. G4: (l) ©Mark Richards/Photo Edit; (r) Gibson Stock Photography. G5: (l) ©Mark Richards/Photo Edit; (r) The Image Bank/Getty Images; (t) ©Macduff Everton/CORBIS. G10: Richard Hamilton Smith/Dembinsky Photo Associates. G12: ©NASA. 1: David Jensen. 3: (b) ©Steve Raymer/CORBIS. 8: (l) Photodisc/Getty Images; (r) D. Berry/PhotoLink/Getty. 9: (l) ©Bruce Coleman Inc./Alamy; (tr) ©Bruce Coleman Inc./Alamy; (br) ©Andrew Slayman/Alamy. 10: Banana Stock/Fotosearch. 12: ©Bob E. Werre/Mira.com. 13: (t) ©Owaki-Kulla/CORBIS; (b) Lawrence Migdale. 14: C.J. Allen/Stock Boston. 16: Dennis Flaherty/AGE Fotostock America. 18: Purpleplanet/Alamy. 19: (t) ThinkStock/Superstock; (b) ©George and Monserrate Schwartz/Alamy. 22: (t) Stock Connection Distribution/Alamy; (b) John Elk III/Elk Photography. 23: (t)LLC,FogStock/Index Stock Imagery; (br) ©Robert Holmes/CORBIS. 24-25: (bkgd) Courtesy of The Bancroft Library, University of California, Berkeley. 25: (t) Michael Melford/The Image Bank/Getty Images. 26: Photodisc/Getty Images. 30: (tr) ©Ron Watts/CORBIS; ©Royalty-Free/CORBIS. 38-39: (bkgd) Arthur S Aubry/Stone+/Getty Images. 40: ©Stockbyte. 41: ©Helen Norman/CORBIS. 42: (cl) ©Paul Barton/CORBIS; (tr) Spencer Grant/Photo Edit; (cr) Maryann Frazier/Photo Researchers. 43: (cl) Gary Conner/Index Stock Imagery; (bl) ©PictureArts/CORBIS; (r) ©Rommel/Masterfile. 44: (bl) Rachel Carson Institute; (tr) ©Underwood & Underwood/CORBIS; (frame) Image Farm Inc. 45: Time Life Pictures/Getty Images. 46-47: (bkgd) ©Eastcott-Momatiuk/The Image Works. 46: (tl) Lawrence Migdale PIX; (bl) Daryl Pederson/Alaska Stock Images. 47: Jeff Schultz/Alaska Stock Images. 48: ©Galen Rowell/CORBIS. 49: Lawrence Migdale PIX. 50: (tl) ©John James/Alamy; (bl) Jean-Pierre Lescourret/Alamy; (br) ©Richard Klune/CORBIS. 51: (t) ©Markus Bassler/Alamy; (b) Tim Hursley/Superstock. 52: Goodshoot/Fotosearch. 57: ©Tom and Dee Ann McCarthy/CORBIS. 58: ©Michael Newman/Photo Edit. 59: (t) Lawrence Migdale/Mira; (b) ©Steve Chenn/CORBIS. 62: (cr) ©John Lei/Omni-Photo Communications. 62: (tl) Michael Newman/Photo Edit. 62: ©John Lei/Omni-Photo Communications; (tl) Michael Newman/Photo Edit. 63: (l) David Paul Morris/Getty Images; AP Photo/Ben Margot. 64: ©Larry Williams/CORBIS. 65: Stockbyte/Getty Images. 66: ©Ariel Skelley/CORBIS. 66-67: (b) Banana Stock/Alamy. 67: Stock Connection Distribution/Alamy. 69: (l) Focus Group/Alamy; (r) ©Charles Gupton/CORBIS. 70-71: Lawrence F. Katzin for MMH. 72: Photodisc/Fotosearch. 75: (tl) Banana Stock/AGE Fotostock; (tr) ©Tom McCarthy/Photo Edit; (b) Jeff Greenberg/Photo Edit. 76: (cl) Greer & Associates, I/AGE Fotostock; (r) Stockbyte/PictureQuest. 77: David Young-Wolff/Photo Edit. 78: ©Royalty-Free/CORBIS. 80: (l) ThinkStock/SuperStock; (r) ©Royalty-Free/CORBIS. 81: (t) ©Bettmann/CORBIS; (b) ©Raymond Bial; (r) Comstock Images/Alamy. 82: Michael Newman/Photo Edit. 83: (t) Vikki Hart/Getty Images; (b) ©Michael Pole/CORBIS. 85: Michael Newman/Photo Edit. 86: Library of Congress, Prints & Photographs Division, LC-DIG-ggbain-02457; (frame) Image Farm Inc. 87: Hulton Archive/Getty Images; (frame) Image Farm Inc. 88: David Young-Wolff/Photo Edit. 89: (l) Don Smetzer/Photo Edit; (cr) Rudi Von Briel/Photo Edit; (br) ©Royalty-Free/CORBIS. 90: (t) ©Ted Soqui/CORBIS; (b) AP/Wide World Photos. 91: (t, b)©Ted Soqui/CORBIS; (c) AP/Wide World Photos. 92: (l) AP Photos/AP-Wide World Photos; (tr) Hulton Archive/Getty Images; (br) Larry Gates/National Museum of American History, Smithsonian Institution. 93: (c) William Lovelace/Hulton Archive/Getty Images; (r) AP-Wide World Photos; (frame) Image Farm Inc. 94: Image Source/Alamy. 95: (t) ©Jennie Woodcock/CORBIS; (c) Arthur Tilley/Getty Images/Taxi. 98-99: (b) ©Alan Oddie/ Photo Edit. 98: (r) Christian Kober/Photo Japan. 99: (c) Brian Fitzgerald/Getty Images; (b) ©Peter Dublin/Stock Boston. 101: Lawrence Migdale/Getty Images. 103: Michael Newman/Photo Edit. 104: (b) Matt Brown. 105: R. Kord/Robertstock/Retrofile. 106: ©Paul Barton/CORBIS. 107: (t) ©Bob Krist/CORBIS; (b) ©Ariel Skelley/CORBIS. 108: ©Ariel Skelley/Masterfile. 108-109: (bkgd) ©Royalty-Free/CORBIS. 110: (tl) Digital Vision Direct; (bl) ©Ariel Skelley/CORBIS; (r) ©Scott Allen/CORBIS. 111: (l) Taxi/Getty Images; (tr) Stock Connection Distribution/Alamy; (br) ©Alan Schein Photography/CORBIS. 112: ©Gary Braasch/CORBIS. 113: (c) ©Michael J. Doolittle/The Image Works; (r) ©NASA. 114-115: (bkgd) ©Rob Crandall/The Image Works; (frame) Image Farm Inc. 115: Elyse Lewin/Photographer's Choice/Getty Images. 116: (l) ©Charles E. Rotkin/CORBIS; (r) The Granger Collection, New York. 117: (t) Hulton Archive/Getty Images; (c) Hulton Archive/Getty Images; (b) Time Life Pictures/Getty Images. 118: ©Bettmann/CORBIS;. 118-119: (c) ©Jeff Vanuga/Westlight/CORBIS; (bkgd) ©Royalty-Free/CORBIS. 119: (t) ©Chase Swift/CORBIS; (b) Brand X Pictures/Alamy. 120: National Museum of American History, Smithsonian Institution, Behring Center. 122: ©Burstein Collection/CORBIS. 123: (l) ©Bettmann/CORBIS; (r) Photodisc/Getty Images. 124: (t) ©Ariel Skelley/CORBIS; (b) A. Ramey/Photo Edit. 125: ©Rob Lewine/CORBIS. 126: (l) Kindra Clineff/Index Stock Imagery; (r) David Toase/Photodisc/Getty Images. 126-127: ©Art Resource, NY/Art Resource. 127: Colonial Williamsburg Foundation . 128-129: Stock Montage. 129: (r) Library of Congress, Prints and Photographs Division. 130-131: North Wind Picture Archives. 131: (t) ©Rick Friedman/CORBIS; (b) Stock Connection Distribution/Alamy. 132-133: Brand X Pictures/Alamy. 133: ©Joseph Sohm/CORBIS. 134: Library of Congress, Prints and Photographs Division. 135: The Granger Collection, New York. 136: (l) The Granger Collection, New York; (r) ©Alan Schein Photography/CORBIS; (frame) Image Farm Inc. 136-137: (bkgd) ©Royalty-Free/CORBIS. 137: (l) ©Kelly-Mooney Photography/CORBIS; (r) The Granger Collection, New York; (frame) Image Farm Inc. 138-139: Getty Images. 140: (l) Hulton Archive/Getty Images; (tr) The Granger Collection, New York; (br) The Granger Collection, New York; (frames) Image Farm Inc. 141: (l) The Granger Collection, New York; (tr) ©Bettmann/CORBIS; (br) Bill Aron/Photo Edit; (frame) Image Farm Inc. 142: ©Joseph Sohm/The Image Works. 143: ©Bettmann/CORBIS. 146: (l) Kevin O'Hara/AGE Fotostock America; (r) Elliot Gerard Daniel/Lonely Planet Images. 147: (t) Comstock Images/Alamy; (b) ©Wolfgang Kaehler/CORBIS. 148: Image State/Alamy. 149: ©Alan Schein Photography/CORBIS. 150: ©Charles E. Rotkin/CORBIS. 153: ©Dorothy Littell Greco/The Image Works. 154: ©Bettmann/CORBIS. 155: (t) Fred Hultstrand History in Pictures Collection, NDIRS-NDSU, Fargo; (b) ©PoodlesRock/CORBIS. 160: (l) ©Phil Schermeister/CORBIS; (r) ©Gabe Palmer/CORBIS. 161: ©Kevin Fleming/CORBIS; (tr) Richard Carroll/Ambient Images. 163: (l) ©O'Brien Productions/CORBIS; (c) ©Gabe Palmer/CORBIS; (r) ©Gabe Palmer/CORBIS. 164: (l) California Historical Society, FN-08033; (r) ©Bettmann/CORBIS. 165: ©Ed Bock/CORBIS. 166: ©Paul Barton/CORBIS. 167: ©Royalty-Free/CORBIS. 170: Joe Sohm/Chromosohm/Stock Connection. 172: ©CORBIS. 172-173: (t) The Granger Collection, New York. 173: ©Ellen Senisi/The Image Works. 174: ©Bettmann/CORBIS; (inset) ©Royalty-Free/CORBIS. 174-175: (inset) ©Royalty-Free/CORBIS. 175: (l) Jeff Dunn/Index Stock Imagery; (r) Siede Preis/Getty Images; (b) ©Gary Houlder/CORBIS. 176: Fred Hultstrand History in Pictures Collection, NDIRS-NDSU, Fargo. 179: Stockbyte Silver Royalty-Free/Getty. 180: (l) Comstock Images/Alamy; (r) AP-Wide World Photos; (frame) Image Farm Inc. 180-181: (b) ©Imagemore/SuperStock. 181: (t) John Sann/Photonica; (b) Nick Short/The State News, Michigan State University. 182-183: ©Seneca Ray Stoddard/CORBIS. 183: Joseph Baylor Roberts/National Geographic/Getty Images. 184: (t) David R. Frazier Photolibrary, Inc./Alamy; (c) ©Vince Streano/CORBIS; (b) David Sanger/Alamy. 186: (t) Photo used with permission from Wells Fargo Bank, N.A.; (b) ©Waldon Fawcett/CORBIS; (frame) Image Farm Inc. 187: (t) The Granger Collection, New York; (b) Andrew McKinney/DK Images. 188-189: Huntington Library/Superstock. 190: (l) David Roth/Getty Images; (r) ©Gabe Palmer/CORBIS. 191: ©Owen Franken/CORBIS. 192-193: ©Danette Rocco Meyer. 194: (l) ©Macduff Everton/CORBIS; (r) ©Werner Forman/CORBIS. 195: (l) ©Danny Lehman/CORBIS; (r) ©Bob Daemmrich/The Image Works. 196: Vintage Images/Alamy; (frame) Image Farm Inc. 197: Taxi/Getty Images. 200: Bruce McMillan. 201: ©Roger Ressmeyer/CORBIS. 202: Taxi/Getty Images. 203: (t) ©Ariel Skelley/CORBIS; (b) ©Royalty-Free/CORBIS. 208: (tl) The Anthony Blake Photo Library/Alamy; © Aileen Ah-Tye. 209: (l) David Young Wolff/Photo Edit; (tr) David Young Wolff/Photo Edit; (br) ©Steve Cole/Masterfile. 210: Photodisc/Getty Images. 211: ©Royalty-Free/CORBIS. 212: ©Ariel Skelley/CORBIS. 213: (t) Stone/Getty Images; (b) ©Ronnie Kaufman/CORBIS. 215: (l) ©Guy Grenier/Masterfile; (r) Barry Winiker/Index Stock Imagery. 216: Mary Kate Denny/Stone/Getty Images. 220: Cindy Charles/Photo Edit. 221: (l) Getty Images; (r) ©James L. Amos/CORBIS. 222: ©Steve Chenn/CORBIS. 224: (l) ©Kelly-Mooney Photography/CORBIS; (r) Pm Images/Stone/Getty Images. 225: ©Richard Hamilton Smith/CORBIS. 226: (t) Steve Mason/Getty Images; (b) David Young-Wolff/Photo Edit. 227: (t) ©John Henley/CORBIS; (b) ©Jeff Zaruba/CORBIS. 228: (t) ©Dan Lamont/CORBIS; (b) David Young-Wolff/Photo Edit. 230: (l) AP-Wide World Photos; (tr) ©Bettmann/CORBIS; (br) Courtesy of the National Park Service; (frame) Image Farm Inc. 231: (l) AP Photo/Nick Ut; (r) ©Mark Peterson/CORBIS. 232: (t) ©Royalty-Free/CORBIS; (b) Getty Images. 233: (t) ©ARS, NY/Art Resource; courtesy of SBC Communications, Inc. Photograph courtesy of Gwendolyn Knight Lawrence; (b) Garry Gay/Photographer's Choice/Getty Images. 234: (l) Photodisc Green/Getty Images; (r) C Squared Studios/Getty Images. 235: (l) ©Royalty-Free/CORBIS; (c) Taxi/Getty Images; (r) Photodisc/Getty Images. 236: (l) David Thurber/AGStock USA; (r) ©Bob Rowan; Progressive Image/CORBIS. 236-237: (bkgd) ©Arthur C. Smith III/Grant Heilman Photography, Inc. 237: (l) ©Royalty-Free/CORBIS; (r) ©Tony Freeman/Photo Edit. 240: (l) Lewis Hine/Granger Collection, New York; (r) Oote Boe/Alamy. 241: (t) ©Bettmann/CORBIS; (b) ©CORBIS. 242: Ron Giling/Peter Arnold, Inc. 242-243: ©Jeremy Horner/CORBIS. 243: ©Ricardo Azoury/CORBIS. 244: ©James L. Amos/CORBIS. 247: ©Ariel Skelley/CORBIS. 249: David Zelick/The Image Bank/Getty Images. 250: ©Reed Kaestner/CORBIS. 251: (t) van hilversum/Alamy; (b) ©Ariel Skelley/CORBIS. 254: (tl) ©Werner Forman/CORBIS; (bl) Joseph Sohm/The Image Works; (r) Jim Oltersdorf/Index Stock Imagery. 255: ©Bettmann/CORBIS. 257: (t) ©Roman Soumar/CORBIS; (b) ©Richard T. Nowitz/CORBIS. 258: ©Bob Krist/CORBIS. 259: Sion Touhig/Getty Images. 260-261: Ariel Skelley/Masterfile. 264: (l) Photri/R.Reed; (r) Edward S. Curtis Collection, Library of Congress; (frame) Image Farm Inc. 264-265: (t) R.P. Kingston/Index Stock Imagery; (c) SHADES OF L.A. ARCHIVES/Los Angeles Public Library. 265: Spencer Grant/Photo Edit. 266: ©Christie's Images/CORBIS. 267: (inset) Peter Ardito/Index Stock Imagery; (r) ©Werner Forman/CORBIS. 268: (l) ©Burstein Collection/CORBIS; (tr) ©CORBIS; (br) Photri/M.Myers. 269: (l) Sequoyah Birthplace Museum; (r) Photri/M.Myers; (frame) Image Farm Inc. 270: (l) ©Museum of the City of New York/CORBIS; (r) The Granger Collection, New York. 271: The Granger Collection, New York. 272: (l) ©National Photo Company/CORBIS; (r) John A. Rizzo/Getty Images. 273: (inset) Comstock Images/Alamy; Michael Zagaris/MLB Photos via Getty Images. 274: (l) Steve Brosnahan Collection of the Lower East Side Tenement Museum; (r) Collection of the Lower East Side Tenement Museum. 275: (l) ©CORBIS. 276: (cr) Kevin Peterson/Photodisc/Getty Images; (b) Mary Evans Picture Library. 277: ©Photo Collection Alexander Alland, Sr./CORBIS. 279: Lewis Hine/The Granger Collection, New York. 282: ©Paul Barton/CORBIS. 283: (t) BananaStock/Fotosearch; (b) ©Michael Newman/PhotoEdit, Inc. 284: (t) James Darell/Royalty-Free/Getty Images; (b) AP/Wide World Photos. 285: David Young Wolff/Photo Edit. 286: Library of Congress, Prints and Photographs Division. 288-289: Yolanda Cater. 290: David Hancock/SkyScans. 290-291: (bkgd) Doug Armand/Stone/Getty Images. 291: ©Burstein Collection/CORBIS. 292: (t) Bryan & Cherry Alexander/Photo Researchers, Inc.; (b) ©Peter Turnley/CORBIS. 294-295: Ariel Skelley/Masterfile. 296: (bl) George Ancona. R1: (l) ©Vince Streano/CORBIS; (c) ©Bob Krist/CORBIS; (r) ©Paul Barton/CORBIS. R4: ©Catherine Karnow/CORBIS. R5: Newell Convers Wyeth/PictureQuest/Wood River Galleries. R6-R7: Ariel Skelley/The Stock Market. R9: (l) Culver Pictures; (r) ©Francis G. Mayer/CORBIS. R10: (l) Arthur Schatz/Time Life Pictures/Getty Images, Inc.; (r) ©Jose Luis Pelaez, Inc./CORBIS. R22: (t to b) The Granger Collection, New York; C.J. Allen/Stock Boston; ©Christie's Images/CORBIS; (bc) ©Paul Barton/CORBIS; Elyse Lewin/Photographer's Choice/Getty Images. R23: (t to b) Andrew Slayman/Alamy; Thinkstock/PictureQuest; ©Reed Kaestner/CORBIS. R24: (t to b) The Granger Collection, New York; ©Joseph Sohm/CORBIS; ©NASA; Digital Vision Direct; ©Rob Lewine/CORBIS. R25: (t to b) The Anthony Blake Photo Library/Alamy; ©Bettmann/CORBIS; Banana Stock/Alamy; ©Phil Schemeister/CORBIS; ©Bettmann/CORBIS. R26: (t to b) ©Rick Friedman/CORBIS; ©Paul Barton/CORBIS; ©Vince Streano/CORBIS; David Young-Wolff/Photo Edit; ©Gabe Palmer/CORBIS. R27: (t to b) ©REUTERS/Adrees Latif/CORBIS; ©Werner Forman/CORBIS; Photodisc/Getty Images; ©Alan Schein Photography/CORBIS; Richard Carroll/Ambient Images; Edward S. Curtis Collection, Library of Congress. R28: (t to b) ©Royalty-Free/CORBIS; ©Bob E. Werre/Mira.com; Bruce Coleman Inc./Alamy; Library of Congress, Prints & Photographs Division, LC-DIG-ggbain-02457; Michael Newman/Photo Edit. R29: (t to b) Arthur Tilley/Getty Images/Taxi; Michael Newman/Photo Edit; Tom McCarthy/Photo Edit; ©Rommel/Masterfile; ©Royalty-Free/CORBIS; ©Steve Cole/Masterfile. R30: (tc) ThinkStock/Superstock; (bc) ©George and Monserrate Schwartz/Alamy. R31: (t to b) Joseph Sohm/The Image Works; David Sanger/Alamy; ©Dan Lamont/CORBIS; Michael Newman/Photo Edit; ©Guy Grenier/Masterfile; ©StockByte; David Young Wolff/Photo Edit.

★ ACKNOWLEDGMENTS ★

Grateful acknowledgment is given to the following authors, composers, and publishers. Every effort has been made to trace the ownership of all copyrighted material and to secure the necessary permissions to reprint these selections. In the case of some selections for which acknowledgment is not given, extensive research has failed to locate the copyright holders.

Big, Beautiful Planet, Words and Music by Raffi Cavourkian. Adapted by Raffi and Louise Dain Cullen. Copyright © 1976 by Homeland Publishing, A Division of Troubadour Music, Inc. International Copyright Secured. All Rights Reserved. Used by Permission.

Always, Rachel: The Letters of Rachel Carson and Dorothy Freeman 1952 – 1964 by Rachel Carson. Copyright © 1994 by Beacon Press. All Rights Reserved. Used by Permission.

Cover permission for **Pipaluk And The Whales**, Text and Illustrations by John Himmelman.Text and Illustrations Copyright © 2001by John Himmelman. Published by National Geographic Society. All Rights Reserved.

Cover permission for **My World & Globe**, Text by Ira Wolfman. Illustrations by Paul Meisel. Copyright © 1991 by Ira Wolfman and Paul Hanson. Cover and Book Illustrations Copyright © 1991 by Paul Meisel. Published by Workman Publishing Company. All Rights Reserved.

Cover permission for **Weather**, created by Pascale De Bourgoing and Gallimard Jeunesse. Illustrations by Sophie Kniffke. (This edition English translation by Christina Cramer. This edition American text by Louise Goldsen) Copyright © 1989 by Editions Gallimard. Published by Scholastic, Inc. All Rights Reserved.

Strength to Love by Martin Luther King, Jr. Copyright © 1963 Augsburg Fortress Publishers. All Rights Reserved. Used by Permission.

Cover permission for **I Have A Dream**, Text by Dr. Martin Luther King, Jr. Illustrations by Fifteen Coretta Scott King Award and Honor Book Artists. Text Copyright © 1963 by Martin Luther King, Jr., Copyright © Renewed 1991by Coretta Scott King. Reprinted by arrangement with The Heirs to the Estate of Martin Luther King, Jr., c/o Writers House Inc. as agent for the proprietor. Published by Scholastic, Inc. All Rights Reserved.

Cover permission for **First Grade Friends: The Lunch Box Surprise**, Text by Grace Maccarone. Illustrations by Betsy Lewin. Text Copyright © 1995 by Grace Maccarone. Illustrations Copyright © 1995 by Betsy Lewin. Activities Copyright © 2003 by Scholastic, Inc. Published by Scholastic, Inc. All Rights Reserved.

Cover permission for **Friends At School**, Text by Rochelle Bunnett. Photographs by Matt Brown. Text Copyright © 1995 by Rochelle Bunnett. Photographs Copyright © 1995 by Matt Brown. Published by Star Bright Books. All Rights Reserved.

Cover permission for **Celebration!**, Text by Jane Resh Thomas. Illustrations by Raul Colon. Text Copyright © 1997 by Jane Resh Thomas. Illustrations Copyright © 1997 by Raul Colon. Published by Hyperion Books For Children. All Rights Reserved.

Cover permission for **Abe Lincoln Remembers**, Text by Ann Turner. Illustrations by Wendell Minor.Text Copyright © 2001 by Ann Turner. Illustrations. Copyright © 2001 by Wendell Minor. Published by HarperCollinsPublishers. All Rights Reserved.

Cover permission for **I Pledge Allegiance**, Text by Bill Martin, Jr. and Michael Sampson. Illustrations by Chris Raschka. Text Copyright © 2002 by Bill Martin, Jr. and Michael Sampson. Illustrations Copyright © 2002 by Chris Raschka. Published by Candlewick Press. All Rights Reserved.

Cover permission for **The Woman Warrior: Memoirs of a Girlhood Among Ghosts**, by Maxine Hong Kingston. Copyright © 1975, 1976 by Maxine Hong Kingston. Published by Random House, Inc. All Rights Reserved. Used by permission.

Conversations with Maxine Hong Kingston edited by Paul Skenazy and Tera Martin. Copyright © 1998 by University Press of Mississippi. All Rights Reserved. Used by Permission.

Cover permission for **When I First Came to This Land**, retold by Harriet Ziefert. Illustrations by Simms Taback. Copyright © 1998 by G.P. Putnam's Sons. All Rights Reserved.

Cover permission for **Grandfather's Trolley**, written and photo-illustrated by Bruce McMillan. Copyright © 1995 by Bruce McMillan. Published by Candlewick Press. All Rights Reserved.

Cover permission for **Homeplace**, Text by Anne Shelby. Illustrations by Wendy Anderson Halperin. Text Copyright © 1995 by Anne Shelby. Illustrations Copyright © 1995 by Wendy Anderson Halperin. Published by Orchard Books, An Imprint of Scholastic, Inc. All Rights Reserved.

Smithsonian Archives of Art, **Interview with Jacob Lawrence** by Caroll Greene. October 16, 1968. Used by Permission.

Cover permission for **Market!**, by Ted Lewin. Copyright © 1996 by Ted Lewin. Published by Lothrop, Lee & Shepard Books. All Rights Reserved.

Cover permission for **Chicken Sunday**, by Patricia Polacco. Copyright © 1992 by Patricia Polacco. Published by PaperStar Books, A Division of the Putnam and Grossett Group. All Rights Reserved.

Cover permission for **Harvesting Hope**, Text by Kathleen Krull. Illustrations by Yuyi Morales. Text Copyright © 2003 by Kathleen Krull. Illustrations Copyright © 2003 by Yuyi Morales. Published by Harcourt, Inc. All Rights Reserved

Lower East Side Tenement Museum, http://www.tenement.org/stoop. Used by Permission.

Cover permission for **Let's Dance**, by George Ancona. Copyright © 1998 by George Ancona. Published by Hampton-Brown. Reprinted by permission of the HarperCollins Children's Books. All Rights Reserved.

Cover permission for **Houses and Homes**, text by Ann Morris. Photographs by Ken Heyman. Text Copyright © 1992 by Ann Morris. Photographs Copyright © 1992 by Ken Heyman. Published by HarperCollins Publishers. All Rights Reserved.

Cover permission for **Coming to America**, Text by Betsy Maestro. Illustrations by Susannah Ryan.Text Copyright © 1996 by Betsy Maestro. Illustrations Copyright © 1996 by Susannah Ryan. Published by Scholastic, Inc. All Rights Reserved.

CALIFORNIA FRAMEWORK

Historical and Social Sciences Analysis Skills

Chronological and Spatial Thinking

1. Students place key events and people of the historical era they are studying in a chronological sequence and within a spatial context; they interpret time lines.

2. Students correctly apply terms related to time, including *past, present, future, decade, century,* and *generation.*

3. Students explain how the present is connected to the past, identifying both similarities and differences between the two, and how some things change over time and some things stay the same.

4. Students use map and globe skills to determine the absolute locations of places and interpret information available through a map's or globe's legend, scale, and symbolic representations.

5. Students judge the significance of the relative location of a place (e.g., proximity to a harbor, on trade routes) and analyze how relative advantages or disadvantages can change over time.

Research, Evidence, and Point of View

1. Students differentiate between primary and secondary sources.

2. Students pose relevant questions about events they encounter in historical documents, eyewitness accounts, oral histories, letters, diaries, artifacts, photographs, maps, artworks, and architecture.

3. Students distinguish fact from fiction by comparing documentary sources on historical figures and events with fictionalized characters and events.

Historical Interpretation

1. Students summarize the key events of the era they are studying and explain the historical contexts of those events.

2. Students identify the human and physical characteristics of the places they are studying and explain how those features form the unique character of those places.

3. Students identify and interpret the multiple causes and effects of historical events.

4. Students conduct cost-benefit analyses of historical and current events.

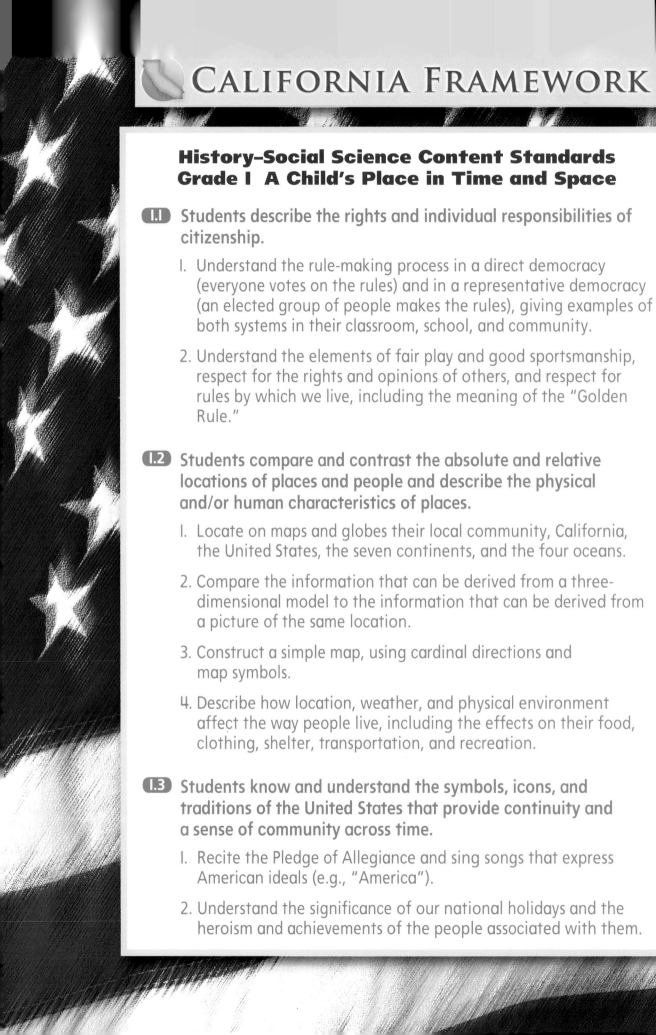

History–Social Science Content Standards
Grade I A Child's Place in Time and Space

I.I Students describe the rights and individual responsibilities of citizenship.

1. Understand the rule-making process in a direct democracy (everyone votes on the rules) and in a representative democracy (an elected group of people makes the rules), giving examples of both systems in their classroom, school, and community.

2. Understand the elements of fair play and good sportsmanship, respect for the rights and opinions of others, and respect for rules by which we live, including the meaning of the "Golden Rule."

I.2 Students compare and contrast the absolute and relative locations of places and people and describe the physical and/or human characteristics of places.

1. Locate on maps and globes their local community, California, the United States, the seven continents, and the four oceans.

2. Compare the information that can be derived from a three-dimensional model to the information that can be derived from a picture of the same location.

3. Construct a simple map, using cardinal directions and map symbols.

4. Describe how location, weather, and physical environment affect the way people live, including the effects on their food, clothing, shelter, transportation, and recreation.

I.3 Students know and understand the symbols, icons, and traditions of the United States that provide continuity and a sense of community across time.

1. Recite the Pledge of Allegiance and sing songs that express American ideals (e.g., "America").

2. Understand the significance of our national holidays and the heroism and achievements of the people associated with them.

3. Identify American symbols, landmarks, and essential documents, such as the flag, bald eagle, Statue of Liberty, U.S. Constitution, and Declaration of Independence, and know the people and events associated with them.

1.4 **Students compare and contrast everyday life in different times and places around the world and recognize that some aspects of people, places, and things change over time while others stay the same.**

1. Examine the structure of schools and communities in the past.

2. Study transportation methods of earlier days.

3. Recognize similarities and differences of earlier generations in such areas as work (inside and outside the home), dress, manners, stories, games, and festivals, drawing from biographies, oral histories, and folklore.

1.5 **Students describe the human characteristics of familiar places and the varied backgrounds of American citizens and residents in those places.**

1. Recognize the ways in which they are all part of the same community, sharing principles, goals, and traditions despite their varied ancestry; the forms of diversity in their school and community; and the benefits and challenges of a diverse population.

2. Understand the ways in which American Indians and immigrants have helped define Californian and American culture.

3. Compare the beliefs, customs, ceremonies, traditions, and social practices of the varied cultures, drawing from folklore.

1.6 **Students understand basic economic concepts and the role of individual choice in a free-market economy.**

1. Understand the concept of exchange and the use of money to purchase goods and services.

2. Identify the specialized work that people do to manufacture, transport, and market goods and services and the contributions of those who work in the home.